RESEARCH PERSPECTIVES IN BUSINESS

ASTERIO T. MIRANDA, JR.,Ph.D.

JUNETH LOURDES F. MIRANDA, CPA, D.M.

ERLINDA G. TEJERO, Ph.D.

RESEARCH PERSPECTIVES IN BUSINESS

Published by CHOA

First Printing, 2018

ISBN 979-11-88425-06-8

We affectionately dedicate this intellectual endeavour to our children: **KAE KAREN CHRISTIE, PEARL JANE DIANNE, JEFF DUSTINN ISHMAEL, MIKAEL GIANN RICK**, and our grandson, **KYRIE.**

We also lovingly dedicate this humble work to **NANAY VERONICA SANCHEZ FIEL, who had been supportive of all our dreams and endeavors.**

JUN and **JUNETH**

My husband, **Pete D. Tejero, Sr**. "the wind beneath my wings'" my children, **Jun** and **Evangeline**, **Zophie Mae** and **Edgar**, **Winston** and **Gina**, **Allison** and **Marife**, **Brando** and **Lisa**, **Anna Darlene, Peter and Michelle Margot, Annalyn Cresta** and **Jerry,** and my grandchildren for providing me "a safe anchor when the sailing gets rough."

LINDA

ACKNOWLEDGMENT

The authors would like to acknowledge the many individuals, authors, editors, publishers, and copyright owners from whom they owe a debt of gratitude. The many significant ways they have helped and contributed to this intellectual endeavor will remain as a legacy for generations to come.

Acknowledgment and endless thanks go to the authors and publishers of books and other materials which have been used and documented in this book. Although most of the selections included in the text have copyrights, it has not proved possible to trace the copyright holders in every case. The authors, editors, and publishers of the materials used are hereby gratefully acknowledged.

The University Administrators of Keimyung University, South Korea for their strong administrative support to Dr. Asterio T. Miranda and Dr. Juneth Lourdes F. Miranda.

To their co-workers and friends from the Keimyung University, South Korea for making their teaching stint in said institution a challenging and memorable one.

The Almighty GOD, the Giver of Life and Source of Everything, who has crafted their very being, their gifts and talents, and who has never ceased to love them despite their inequities and sinfulness.

The Authors

TABLE OF CONTENTS

LIST OF FIGURES

LIST OF APPENDICES

MODULE 1

GETTING STARTED

FOCUS QUESTIONS:

After reading this instructional module, the student shall be able to answer the following questions:

1. What will you do to improve your research skills, in general?
2. What will you do to improve your research skills related to business;
3. What study plan on the use of this book will you present? and
4. What issues related to research will you raise when interacting with your fellow students?

GETTING STARTED

Introduction

The 21st Century ushered in a fast-paced and highly competitive modern world. To survive and be a significant contributor to the cause of knowledge and live effectively in this complex world, you must possess survival skills for global competitiveness. Without these skills, you will be left out in the race while others are scampering to reach the heights of their ambition and careers. Skill in language and communication, particularly in the use of the English is one of them. Language, is not only desired but has now become a necessity. English, being the international language, must be learned and learned well. Language incompetence will put you far behind your contemporaries who are very articulate and proficient in its usage. Passing an oral interview is one determining factor in landing a good job or pursuing a career. Establishing connections and being able to approach people will mean a lot of difference in your search for the good life. Language skill is thus very crucial in your quest for knowledge, in your search for better jobs, and in establishing good business linkages with other people.

To be proficient in the use of English brings a lot of advantages. Businessmen can make a difficult deal come through and be successful with appropriate language use. Professionals can look a lot more professional when they are proficient in the language of communication. The quest for knowledge found in hidden treasures like the books will be a lot easier if one is proficient in the language used in writing them.

Research is another important survival skill. It is akin to life. It is helpful in identifying your life's problems and finding solutions to them. This book provides you with significant knowledge and insights about research, in general and business research, in particular. While this book can be a good reference on the subject in Business Research, this can also be useful as a material for your self-improvement program.

This book, **RESEARCH PERSPECTIVES IN BUSINESS** is the answer to your learning needs along this determination. But you should not only read this now and forget all about it. Then after a year, you remember you bought one and try to locate it because it seems it cannot be seen somewhere in your vicinity of things. When you resolve to buy this book and decided that this is the answer to your dilemma, then make sure you will use it for your self-improvement program, should you desire to do so.

Now, first things first. Set a goal to implement your self-improvement program then use this book. The goal will steer you toward the direction you want to go – and that is to improve your proficiency in research activities. If by chance, you are already proficient in the subject of research, you can still decide to achieve more. Anyway, there is always a big room for improvement, so they say.

Setting a Goal

A goal, in this context, is the end result which you wish to achieve for yourself after a period of time. The time frame may be a few months, a year, or longer. It depends on how fast you are able to work on it.

For instance, you are a fast learner and you feel you will be able to attain your goal in a few month's time, say, four months at the most. Or you can decide to finish it in six-month's time because you are too busy at the moment. Your work schedule is such that you feel you are strait-jacketed to it. To decide to study using this book during your time for rest wouldn't just work. Competing schedules and your self-improvement program are now at opposite odds. You should really decide what to do first. Prioritization of things and workload within your sphere will be needed. And whatever you decide, managing your time is of primary concern to you.

Managing Your Time

Bennett (1991) averred that time is of the essence. He says that many people seem to be caught alternately at both ends of a contradictory scale. Others would say, "There is never enough time," (a sigh of frustration). Some would say, "There is nothing to do," (a sigh of boredom).

He cited the obstacles to good time management: (1) Overconfidence; (2) Insecurity; (3) Taking things for granted; (4) Closing one's mind.

According to him, as you go through life – becoming more mature, becoming educated, becoming personally responsible for yourself and your actions, things become more complex. You feel there is more to do, there are more places to visit, more demands are made on your time and your talents, and the penalties of failure are greater. There is too much to handle. Confidence is good but overconfidence is not. Proper time management requires planning and thought. Others feel insecure because they have limited abilities and that leads them to bolt out. This is the attitude of a defeatist. The object is to always try to do your best and being prepared will help you overcome feelings of insecurity. Do not take things for granted. The best weapon when ready to attack is being well-prepared. Closing one's mind is not good. You can always learn from others no matter how naïve they are. Good things sometimes happen from things you least expect to happen.

A good strategy in managing your time is to plan a schedule and budget your time. If possible make a calendar of your activities so that you don't miss out on important things to do and appointments to attend to.

You may like to adopt this example. Fill in the date every time you sit down to study.

Day	Date	Topics
________	________	Module 1 Getting Started
________	________	Module 2 Overview of Research
________	________	Module 3 The Research Problem
________	________	Module 4 The Review of Related Literature and Studies
________	________	Module 5 The Research Methodology
________	________	Module 6 Statistical Treatment of Data
________	________	Module 7 Presentation, Analysis and Interpretation of Data
________	________	Module 8.Summary, Conclusions and Recommendations
________	________	Module 9.Documentation and Bibliography
________	________	Module 10. Guidelines for Writing Research Report
________	________	Module 11. Models of Research Reports

MODULE 2

OVERVIEW OF RESEARCH

FOCUS QUESTIONS:

After studying this instructional module, the students shall be able to answer the following questions:

1. What is social science research?
2. What are the aims and purposes of social science research?
3. What are the facets of social science research?
4. What are the stages of social science research?
5. What is business research?
6. What are the purposes of business research?

Research Defined

Research is a very important facet in the life of man. Being a continuous search for the unknown, man is able to discover many unknown facts and realities through research. Research enables man to forward the cause of knowledge and arrive at this present highly technological and modern world.

What then is research? Social science research is the systematic observation, documentation, and analysis of social phenomena. It entails the measurement, classification, analysis and interpretation of social facts for the purpose of understanding underlying trends and patterns in social phenomena, as well as their causes and consequences. It aims to arrive at generalizations based on the empirical observation of social phenomena and formulate theories that explain various aspects of social life, relationships and functioning.

Generally, social science research is intended to explore answers to questions about a social phenomenon through a systematic, objective, and comprehensive investigation, thereby raising the level of knowledge and understanding of the social world.

Social science research has many facets. It is empirical, propositional, logical, operational, public, objective, self-correcting and cumulative.

- Empirical. It rests on data; it is concerned with a knowable real world. Scientific claims must be assessed on the basis of evidence. It involves testing and retesting in an effort to discover the validity and the limits of propositions or the conditions under which they or they may not hold.

- Propositional. It deals with statements which share a truth-value about things, but these propositions may be rejected or modified in the future (its assumptions, definitions and procedural rules are all subject to re-examination.)

- Logical. It makes use of the rules of logic in reasoning and drawing conclusions and inferences. The structure of a scientific argument follows the rules of logic.

- Operational. While logic is completely formal, science requires that its logical arguments are connected with reference to specific aspects of the real world. The process of establishing the connection and correspondence between logical and abstract thinking with that which is empirical or directly observable is termed as "operational procedure".

- Public. Science can be communicated from one scientist to another. Symbols utilized in science must be well represented for the scientists to judge the correctness of the inferences drawn. This allows other scientists to replicate any research study.

- Objective. Scientific inquiry is marked by impartiality and disinterestedness. Scientists are expected to be objective and to have no vested interest in their findings.

- Self – correcting and Cumulative. Because scientific research studies can be replicated, the social science research process offers a system of revalidating available findings under different times and circumstances, and therefore of correcting and improving on existing knowledge.

There are ten stages of social science research, as follows:

Stage 1: Social Problem/Theory. The research always starts with a problem felt by people or individuals in a social setting. The problem is actually a "gap" between "what is" and "what ought to be". This concept may be illustrated as follows:

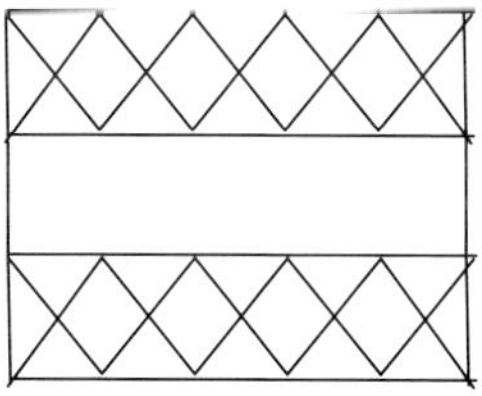

what is" the actual situation?

gap/problem

"what ought to be" the ideal situation

When a research is conducted to solve the problem, the "gap" is then filled. New knowledge evolves through the conduct of research. The illustration for this concept follows:

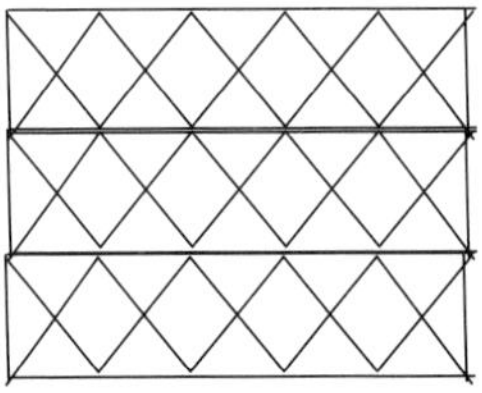

The "gap" has already been filled, the problem solved and new knowledge had been evolved.

For instance, a problem about the deterioration of values among the businessmen is felt by the people in the community. This seemingly low level of values among them results in opportunism, dishonesty in business dealings, immorality, promiscuity, disrespect for law and order, and the like. General questions relative to the problem at hand may be raised:

1. Why do some businessmen exhibit undesirable values?
2. Why do they misbehave or commit crimes?
3. Why is it that some businessmen are well behaved while others are not?
4. What might be the causes of their undesirable values and criminal tendencies or acts?
5. Are there solutions to these societal problems?

Stage 2: The Research Problem. The social problems identified in stage 1 are too broad in scope. So the problem statement should be narrowed–down to zero–in on a specific research problem in a specific setting. Questions relative to the problem may be raised.

1. Are the problems related to the businessmen's undesirable values also felt in the local setting of the study?

2. To what extent are these problems felt?
3. What may be their causes?
4. What recommendations can be proposed to minimize, if not solve the problems?
5. Thus, from the problem statement, research questions are formulated.

Stage 3: Research Goals and Objectives. The goals and objectives of the research are then stated. The goals of a specific research study are broader in scope. These are translated into more specific terms. These become the objectives of the study. The objectives of the study are stated in behavioral terms following the acronym **SMART**:

- **S**pecific – the research tackles a specific problem in a specific setting at a specific time.
- **M**easurable – there is a way of measuring the constructs or concepts.
- **A**ttainable – there is the possibility of achieving what you intend to do at the start of the research.
- **R**esult–oriented – the research should yield results that will be useful to the proponent, the research locale, and society in general.
- **Ti**me–bounded – the research undertaking should be accomplished within the time frame specified for its completion.

Stage 4: Theoretical/Conceptual Framework. The Theoretical/ Conceptual Framework indicates all the constructs (concepts, definitions, and propositions) that relate to the problem. The problem is hinged to a theory or theories. These theories are then operationalized in the context of the study.

1. Are the problems also felt in the local setting of the study?
2. To what extent are the problems felt?
3. What may be the causes of the problems?

Stage 5: Research Questions/Hypothesis. The hypotheses to be tested are formulated based on the research problems.

Stage 6: Data Collection. Using different research tools, the data are collected. Data may be collected through the triangulation method employing questionnaires, interview, observation and documentary analysis.

Stage 7: Data Processing and Analysis. To gather the raw data, the research instruments are scored, tabulated, computed, and analyzed.

Stage 8: Data Interpretation. Interpretations of data are based on inferences and deductions on documented evidences, supporting or contradicting the findings of the study and on the researcher's insightful interpretation using implications and synthesis.

Stage 9: Summary and Conclusions. Resume of the major findings which answer each sub-problem and hypothesis is formulated.

Stage 10: Implications and Recommendations. What the findings imply or mean and what suggestions can be given to improve the status or condition being studied are given.

Research, being a cyclical process, starts with a problem and a theory and ends up comparing the findings against the theory, whether they confirm or contradict it.

The stages of social science research are illustrated in Figure 1 below:

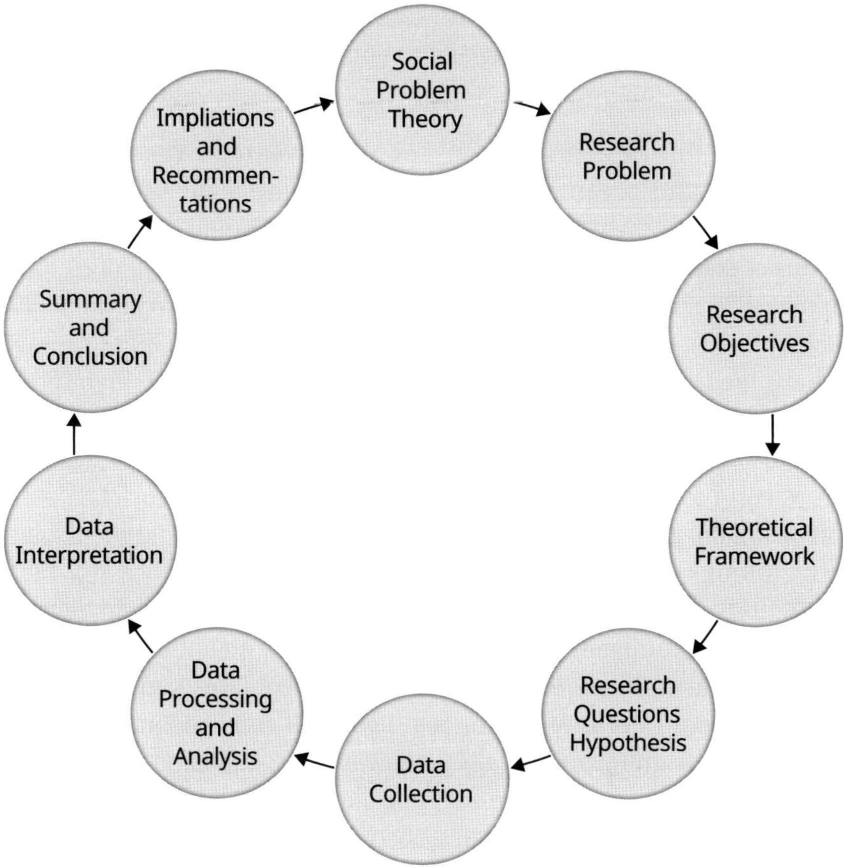

Fig. 1. Stages of Social Science Research

What is Business Research?

Research can be undertaken in many areas or fields such as in education, environment, health, legal, business, engineering, agriculture, etc. Conducting research in business and economics will forward the cause of knowledge along that line and thus, improve the life and living of the people.

What then is business research? The following presentation is aimed at equipping the students of business the rudiments of business research to enable them to gain knowledge about it, improve the quality of their lives and be ready to contribute their share in nation building.

Sekaran and Bougie (2013) describe business research as a systematic and organized effort to investigate a specific problem encountered in the work setting, which needs solution. It comprises a series of steps that are designed and executed with the goal of finding answers to the issues that are of concern to the manager in the work environment. This means that the first step in research is to know where the problem areas exist in the organization, and to identify as clearly and specifically as possible the problems that need to be studied and resolved. Once a problem that needs attention is clearly defined, steps can be taken to determine the factors that are associated with the problem, gather information, and analyze the data and then solve it by taking the necessary corrective measures. This process which attempts to solve problems, is called research. Thus research involves a series of well-thought-out and carefully executed activities that enable the manager to know how organizational problems can be solved, or at least considerably minimized. Research thus encompasses the processes of inquiry, investigation, examination, and experimentation. These processes have to be carried out systematically, diligently, critically, objectively and logically. The expected end result would be a discovery that helps the manager to deal with the problem situation.

In view of their foregoing insights, they arrived at the definition of business research as an *organized, systematic, data-based, critical, objective, inquiry or investigation into a specific problem, undertaken with the purpose of finding answers or solutions to it.* According to them, research must be able to provide the necessary information that will guide the managers to make informed decisions to successfully deal with problems. These information could be the result of a careful analysis of data gathered first-hand or of data that are already available. These can be ***quantitative***, data that are in the form of numbers as generally gathered through structured questions, or

qualitative, data in the form of words as generated from the broad answers to questions in interviews, or from responses to open-ended questions in questionnaire, or through observation, or from already available information gathered from various sources such as the Internet.

Purposes of Business Research

Burke (2014) stated that **b**usiness research is important for determining the viability of new products and services. Businesses use research to set themselves apart from their competition in various ways. It can provide valuable information on consumer buying habits, for example, giving data on attitudes to products and brands. Research is especially important for people who want to launch a start-up, as it helps them assess if an idea can support a new business.

He explained each purpose, as follows:

1. **Using Research to Evaluate Start-up Viability**. Market research allows entrepreneurs to base the viability of their business ideas on facts instead of enthusiasm. People can get excited about starting a business that focuses on their interests, but research helps determine if there is a big enough market to support a prospective business and make it profitable. Reports done by government agencies, trade associations and market research firms can help entrepreneurs spot market trends and determine who might buy their products and services.

2. **Using Research to Estimate Costs**. Businesses, especially new ones, often cost more than their owners anticipate. Nonetheless, research is needed to estimate at least a year's worth of business expenses to create a budget. You won't be able to set the correct prices for your products and services or turn a profit if you don't know how much it costs to run your business. Your research should include things such as the cost of insurance, business licenses and product packaging.

3. **Using Research to Set Prices**. Research helps businesses get a handle on pricing and prevents them from pushing themselves out of the market by setting prices too high. Some of this research includes tracking competitors' prices. That not only involves examining how much competitors charge for products and services, but it also includes noting the features or extras they offer. You might be selling a product that costs more than similar items. However, if customers can do more with your product compared with others, that might constitute a selling point that justifies not lowering your price.

4. **Using Research to Analyze Competitors**. Businesses also can size up their competitors with consumer research. Examine competitors' blogs, social networking sites and websites. Take note of any comments that consumers post on your competitors' sites, paying close attention to negative and positive responses about products and services. Consider how your business can outshine competitors based on those customer comments. Visiting competitors' stores is another way to research the competition. Examine the store layout, then note whether it's easy to find products and whether the store feels cramped or cluttered. Also note the mix of products, and determine how your product inventory compares with your competitors' inventory.

REVIEW QUESTIONS

1. What is social science research?

2. What are the aims and purposes of social science research?

3. What are the facets of social science research? Make a synthesis of each facet.

4. What are the stages in social science research? Explain each stage.

5. What is business research?

6. What are the purposes of business research?

MODULE 3

THE RESEARCH PROBLEM

FOCUS QUESTIONS:

After studying this instructional module, the students are expected to answer the following questions:

1. Why is research important?
2. What are the conditions that point to the existence of a problem?
3. What are the characteristics of a good research problem?
4. What are the sources of a research problem?
5. What are the facets of a business research?
6. What is the importance of conducting business research?
7. How is a research problem in business identified?

THE RESEARCH PROBLEM

Why Research?

Research, in general, is done for three main purposes. It may be done to **search for a theory**. In qualitative research, common patterns related to specific issues, groups, or areas of interest to researchers, agencies, and communities are noted and made as bases for a new theory that may emerge. In quantitative research, numerical measures are employed in data analysis in order to **test a theory.** Findings of the investigation are compared against the theory, whether they confirm or negate it. Research may also be done **to solve a problem.** The problem is not an ordinary one. It is something which could not be dealt with easily such as not having enough money for one's needs. This problem does not need a full blown research in order to solve it. One only needs to do some kind of profitable work to generate income. The research problem referred to here is something that needs to be solved using scientific procedures. This is aptly termed as scientific research.

Kerlinger defines scientific research as a systematic, controlled, empirical, and critical investigation of hypothetical propositions about presumed relations among natural phenomena. Scientific research is systematic because it follows steps or stages in the process. It starts with the identification of the problem, relating the problem to existing theories, formulating hypotheses, data gathering, analysis, and interpretation, formulating conclusions and implications, and recommendations for further improvement and finally the findings and conclusions form part of the existing body of knowledge. In this instance, research has done its job of forwarding the cause of knowledge. Research is controlled because variables are manipulated, classified, and categorized based on the purposes or aims of the study. It is empirical because it is based on data gathered at the time of the study. It is a critical investigation involving in-depth analysis of natural phenomena and employs higher-order thinking skills of the researcher.

Identifying the Research Problem

When a problem does exist? A problem exists:

1. when there is an absence of information resulting in a "gap" in knowledge;
2. when there are contradictory results; and
3. when a fact exists and you intend to make your study explain it.

What are the characteristics of good problems? (McGingan: 1978).

First, a good problem should be of great interest to you. Research is a long and arduous process. To do it you need to be highly motivated and interested. Pursuing something difficult would be futile, if and when interest and motivation is lacking or absent.

Second, it should be useful for the concerned people in a particular field. This is why, you as the researcher, should select a topic within your field of endeavour so that you can share the benefits of your research work with the other people in that particular field of interest.

Third, it should be novel. Your research topic should be something new so that you can be sure that it really contributes to the formation of new knowledge and not just a mere repetition of what has been done already.

Fourth, it should lend itself to complex designing. Complex research designs demand more rigorous work and in-depth analysis. From these, better results can be expected.

Fifth, it should be completed in the allotted time desired. Do not delay your research work because timeliness and freshness of your data and findings will be crucial. Finish your research work within the time frame you have set at the start.

Sixth, it should not carry ethical or moral impediments. The ethics of research demand that you do not intrude into the personal lives of your respondents, unless allowed to do so. Generally, ethical and moral considerations should be held high. Your research will fail if your respondents will refuse to answer questions related to ethical and moral issues (Sevilla, et al.:1992).

Sources of a Problem

There are many sources of problems. There are many sources of research problems. One of the best sources of research problems is the national research agenda of every country. For example in the Philippines, research topics could be identified from the National Higher Education Research Agenda (NHERA) of the Commission on Higher Education (CHED). The research priority of CHED is spelled out in the NHERA publication. This includes the gaps of knowledge identified by CHED which need to be studied and which will be the basis for policy formulation.

Other sources of a research problem may be derived from the following: (1) experiences and observations; (2) the vast amount of literature in your own field; (3) courses that you have taken; (4) journals, books, magazines, or abstracts; (5) theses and dissertation (focused on recommendations); (6) your professors and your classmates; and (7) the internet.

Formulating the Research Problem

Reviewing what is already known about a problem situation through the search for related literature and studies is an essential part of the research process. A good review of information will suggest the social, economic, political, cultural and historical aspects of the problem. This will help to narrow the focus of the proposed investigation. It will indicate the major theoretical concepts and operational variables other researchers have considered important. It will suggest possible research hypotheses that need to be tested and it will help the researcher avoid the areas of study which have already been explored by other researchers many times over.

Suggested Topics for Business Research

Topics for research may vary depending on the researcher's need. As published by Midway College, topics may fall under major sub-headings such as business, education, environment, government policy, health, human behavior, legal issues, media and freedom of speech, religion, social issues, and the world.

Some examples of topics for business research are suggested:

1. **Cheap labor:** U.S. companies that move factories to undeveloped nations barely pay employees enough to live on. Is it unethical to pay cheap wages or are companies doing those workers a favor?
2. **Fitness programs:** Should companies allow employees to exercise on work time?
3. **Mining:** What safety measures made the recent Canadian mining accident a noncasualty event, while recent U.S. mining accidents have been fatal?
4. **Oil companies:** Do oil companies make big bucks while the rest of us pay over $3 a gallon?
5. **Wage gap:** Women still earn only 75 cents for every $1 a man earns. Explain why.
6. **Wages:** There's a minimum wage, but should there also be a maximum wage/salary a person can earn?
7. **Workaholics:** Do Americans work too hard? Does working more actually reduce productivity? Is a 40-hour workweek too much? Should there be a mandatory cap on the number of hours a person can work? Should there be changes in employment laws to give Americans more relaxation time?

REVIEW QUESTIONS

1. What are the purposes of research?

2. Why is there a need to conduct business research?

3. How is scientific research defined?

4. How is scientific research defined?

5. What is business research?

6. What are the purposes of business research?

MODULE 4

REVIEW OF RELATED LITERATURE AND STUDIES

FOCUS QUESTIONS

After studying this instructional module, the students are expected to answer the following:

1. What is the significance of a good literature review?
2. How would you distinguish between conceptual and research literature?
3. What are the four types of entry references in reviewing related literature?
4. What is a theory?
5. How would you differentiate the theoretical framework from the conceptual framework?
6. How are terms defined?
7. What is a research hypothesis and how are they formulated?
8. How are related studies selected and cited?
9. What are the important details cited in comparing the similarities and differences of the present study and those reviewed?

Review of Related Literature

No one has yet written a thesis or dissertation worthy of its name without undertaking a good literature search or review.

A literature review, according to Taylor, (2014) is an account of what has been published on a topic by accredited scholars and researchers. Occasionally you will be asked to write one as a separate assignment (sometimes in the form of an annotated bibliography—see the bottom of the next page), but more often it is part of the introduction to an essay, research report, or thesis. In writing the literature review, your purpose is to convey to your reader what knowledge and ideas have been established on a topic, and what their strengths and weaknesses are. As a piece of writing, the literature review must be defined by a guiding concept (e.g., your research objective, the problem or issue you are discussing or your argumentative thesis). It is not just a descriptive list of the material available, or a set of summaries.

Besides enlarging your knowledge about the topic, writing a literature review lets you gain and demonstrate skills in two areas:

1. **Information seeking**: the ability to scan the literature efficiently, using manual or computerized methods, to identify a set of useful articles and books; and
2. **Critical appraisal:** the ability to apply principles of analysis to identify unbiased and valid studies.

A literature review must do these things: 1)be organized around and related directly to the thesis or research question you are developing; 2)synthesize results into a summary of what is and is not known; 3)identify areas of controversy in the literature; and 4).formulate questions that need further research.

On a personal note, the researcher may ask questions like these: 1) what is the specific thesis, problem, or research question that my literature review helps to define? 2) what type of literature review am

I conducting? Am I looking at issues of theory? methodology? policy? quantitative research (e.g. on the effectiveness of a new procedure)? qualitative research (e.g., studies)? 3)what is the scope of my literature review? What types of publications am I using (e.g., journals, books, government documents, popular media)? What discipline am I working in (e.g., nursing psychology, sociology, and medicine)? 4) how good was my information seeking? Has my search been wide enough to ensure I've found all the relevant material? Has it been narrow enough to exclude irrelevant material? Is the number of sources I've used appropriate for the length of my paper? 5)have I critically analyzed the literature I use? Do I follow through a set of concepts and questions, comparing items to each other in the ways they deal with them? Instead of just listing and summarizing items, do I assess them, discussing strengths and weaknesses? 6) have I cited and discussed studies contrary to my perspective? 7) will the reader find my literature review relevant, appropriate, and useful?

Ask yourself questions like these about each book or article you include:

1. Has the author formulated a problem/issue?
2. Is it clearly defined? Is its significance (scope, severity, relevance) clearly established?
3. Could the problem have been approached more effectively from another perspective?
4. What is the author's research orientation (e.g., interpretive, critical science, combination)?
5. What is the author's theoretical framework (e.g., psychological, developmental, feminist)?
6. What is the relationship between the theoretical and research perspectives?

7. Has the author evaluated the literature relevant to the problem/issue? Does the author include literature taking positions she or he does not agree with?

8. In a research study, how good are the basic components of the study design (e.g., population, intervention, outcome)? How accurate and valid are the measurements? Is the analysis of the data accurate and relevant to the research question? Are the conclusions validly based upon the data and analysis?

9. In a material written for a popular readership, does the author use appeals to emotion, one-sided examples, or rhetorically-charged language and tone? Is there an objective basis to the reasoning, or is the author merely "proving" what he or she already believes?

10. How does the author structure the argument? Can you "deconstruct" the flow of the argument to see whether or where it breaks down logically (e.g., in establishing cause-effect relationships)?

11. In what ways does this book or article contribute to our understanding of the problem under study, and in what ways is it useful for practice? What are the strengths and limitations?

12. How does this book or article relate to the specific thesis or question I am developing?

Extensive readings on the topic or problem are necessary in order for you to know your entry point to the topic. The PSSC (2000) gave additional insights on the value of conducting a good literature search enumerated below:

- Helps in identifying a research problem;
- Helps in defining or refining a research problem;

- Avoids unnecessary duplication of previous works;
- Offers the researcher a range of theoretical and conceptual frameworks, debates, and issues about the research topic;
- Provides information about what variables have been investigated so far, the research methods used, and how the findings were interpreted;
- Allows the researcher to foresee significant directives and issues; and
- Suggests how the planned research can contribute to enriching what is currently known. (PSSC: 2000).

When undertaking your review of related literature and studies, it is advisable to use index cards. The use of index cards lends to flexibility in the arrangement or logical sequencing of your research materials.

Four types of entry reference notes may be employed as follows:

1. Quotation. The exact words of an author are reproduced and enclosed in quotation marks. It is important to copy each statement verbatim and to indicate the exact page reference so that quotations can be properly documented in the written report.
2. Paraphrase. You can restate the author's thoughts in your own words.
3. Summary. You can restate in condensed form the contents of the article.
4. Evaluation. You can record your reaction indicating agreement or disagreement or interpreting the point of view of the writer (PSSC : 2000)

There are two types of literature that you are going to search or review – the conceptual literature and the research literature. The conceptual literature or related literature pertains to articles or books written by authorities giving their opinions, experiences, theories or ideas of what is good or bad, desirable and undesirable within the problem area. Research literature or related studies refers to published or unpublished reports on actual research studies done previously.

Sources of Conceptual Literature:

1. Encyclopedia of the Social Sciences – provides synopsis of progress in the fields of social science, including education, law, philosophy and statistics.
2. Other encyclopedias such as Encyclopedia Britannica, Encyclopedia Americana, World Book Encyclopedia, Collier's Encyclopedia, International Encyclopedia o f the Social Sciences, Book of knowledge, etc.
3. Yearbooks and handbooks such as the World Almanac, Statesman's Yearbook, Philippine Yearbook, and Philippine Statistical Yearbook.

Sources of Research Literature:

1. Theses and dissertations
2. Abstracts such as the Social Science Abstracts, Dissertation Abstracts, International Abstracts, Historical Abstracts, Geographical Abstracts, Sociological Abstracts, Psychological Abstracts, etc.
3. International and National Social Science Journal,
4. International Social Science Journal, Journal of International Economic Studies, Philippine Journal of Psychology, Philippine Journal of Public Administration, etc.

Theory Defined

Your literature search should include primarily the search for a theory that would link your topic to an available body of knowledge. This is usually done in quantitative research or researches involving numerical data.

Kerlinger defines theory as a set of interrelated constructs (concepts), definitions and propositions that present a systematic view of phenomena by specifying relations among variables, with the purpose of predicting the phenomena.

Examples of a theory:

1. A theory on personality development developed by Argyris (1978: 56–57) suggests that in one culture, personality develops from an immature to mature state through changes in these aspects of the self:

    a. from passivity to activity (doing for oneself rather than having others do for one)

    b. from dependence to independence (from seeking direction to liking autonomy)

    c. from inflexible to flexible behavior (ability to change and adopt)

    d. from shallow interest to deep interest (finding satisfaction and reward in doing something for its own sake)

    e. from short perspective to long-term perspective (pursuing a long – term goal by a series of steps to the goal)

    f. from accepting subordination to desiring equality or superiority

    g. to peers (seeking at least an equal voice in determining one's activity)

    h. from lack of control to self–control (ability to direct oneself without external control)

2. A theory on motivation postulated by Reitz (1981:73-74) states that people are capable of being motivated by a large, complete set of motives or reinforcers which deal with physiological survival, security, affiliation, esteem, self–actualization, achievement, competence, security, activity, and beauty. The range and variety of these factors make it imperative to account for individual differences in the strength of individual responses to a given reward.

3. The Law of Effect advocated by Thorndike speaks of the tendency of the organism to react to a particular way to given situations. It signifies the degree of probability that a certain response will be made under stimulating conditions (Aquino, et al : 1985 : 105-115).

   The theory performs some functions such as the following:

   a. It identifies the start for the research problem by presenting the gaps, weak points, and inconsistencies in the previous researches. This provides the study with a conceptual framework justifying the need for investigation.

   b. Its puts together all the constructs or concepts that are related with the research topic. The theory then leads you into the specific questions to ask in your investigation.

   c. It presents the relationships among variables that have been investigated. This process enables you to view the topic on hand against the findings earlier bared. These findings have the function of explaining the phenomena. (Sevilla, et al. 1992 : 45-46).

Specifically, for business research, management theories such as Administrative Management Theories, Scientific Management Theories, Motivational Theories, etc. may be selected depending on their applicability to the research proposed.

Theoretical/Conceptual Framework

Once a theory or theories are found that would link your topic to a body of knowledge, you now formulate your theoretical framework. The theoretical framework serves as the structural frame or base of your study. The core theory should relate to the major variable of your study and the other supporting theories should be linked to the other research variables. The theories are then made operational in the conceptual frame of the study.

The presentation of the theories and how they operate in the study should be such that they dovetail with the variables to be studied.

The Hypothesis

You then proceed to explain the relationship between variables through the statement of the hypothesis. A hypothesis is a tentative explanation for certain behaviors, phenomena or events which have occurred or will occur. It is the most specific statement of a problem. It provides a translation of the problem into a form more amenable to testing.

A good hypothesis possesses certain characteristics:

1. A good hypothesis is researchable;
2. It should be stated in declarative form;
3. It should state, in definite terms, the relationships between the variables;
4. It should be testable;
5. It should follow the findings of previous studies.
6. It should be related to a body of theory

The null hypothesis (Ho) means there is no existence of an effect, an interaction of relationship or of difference. The alternative hypothesis

(Ha) is considered the operational statement of the research hypothesis

A comparison of the characteristics of the null and alternative hypothesis is presented.

The Null Hypothesis or Statistical Hypothesis	Research Hypothesis
• Always a statement of equality or no relationship • Always refers to the population • Since the entire population cannot be directly tested, the null hypothesis must be indirectly tested through the research hypothesis • Always stated using Greek letters	• Always a statement of inequality or relationship • Always refers to a sample • Tested directly • Always stated using Roman symbols • Can be directional or non-directional

For more examples, please see Salkind's versions of five research hypotheses in the appendices.

Definition of Terms

In the search for literature, you also list the key terms in your study and define these terms conceptually and operationally. A differentiation of the two types of definition is given:

Conceptual definition is the universal or academic meaning attributed to a word or group of words. These can be found in books, encyclopedia, magazines, and journals.

Operational definition is also known as the functional definition. The terms are defined based on the conceptual definition and operationalized in the context of the study.

Related Studies

The related studies are also called research literature. The purpose of reviewing research literature is for you to know what have been done in the field in relation to your topic. This way, you will know what have already been explored, what needs to be explored, and what topic is over explored. This will guide you in deciding which topic to pursue. It is not advisable to select over explored topics although it may still hold some merits such as replicating studies in different places involving different respondents and research methodologies in order to prove the generalizability of the previous studies. Topics which are unexplored or least explored should be selected so that after you have conducted your study you have somehow contributed your share in forwarding the cause of knowledge and not just a mere repetition of what have already been said and done by others.

Unpublished studies may be found in the libraries of schools offering graduate studies. A big collection of these studies can also be found in the National Libraries.

Note taking is an important skill which you should develop. You should know what to get in your search for research literature. Do not be remiss in getting the important facts of the studies you will be reviewing because if you do, it will be difficult for you to go back to the materials all over again. The general guidelines for writing thesis proposals and dissertation protocols found in Module VIII of this book will be a good reference on what to get, where to go, and what to do during your search for related studies.

Similarities and Differences

After your related studies, there is a portion that points out the similarities and differences of the studies cited and your present study. A good advice will be for you to cite first the similarities followed by the differences. Some schools require their students to have this immediately after each study is cited. Other schools require their students to have a separate section for presenting similarities and differences. Whichever style you use is acceptable depending on the requirements of the specific school.

REVIEW QUESTIONS

1. Why is the review of related literature and studies important?

2. What are the characteristics of a good review of related literature?

3. Differentiate conceptual literature from research literature.

4. What is a theory? Give examples of a theory.

5. Differentiate theoretical framework from a conceptual framework.

6. Give example of a null hypothesis.

7. What are the four types of entry references in reviewing related literature?

8. What are the important details cited in comparing the similarities and differences of the present study and those reviewed?

MODULE 5

THE RESEARCH METHODOLOGY

FOCUS QUESTIONS:

After studying this instructional module the students are expected to answer the following questions:

1. How do you differentiate a research design from research methods?
2. How do you explain exploratory, descriptive, and experimental studies?
3. What is the nature and characteristics of quasi – experimental research designs?
4. What are the different sampling techniques?
5. How do you compute the sample size of a particular research population?
6. What are the guidelines for questionnaire construction?
7. What other research methodologies may be used for conducting business research?

Research Designs

A research design is the arrangement of conditions for the collection and analysis of data that is relevant to and will best address the research purpose and with the minimum expenditure of effort, money, and time.

The design of your research depends primarily on the nature of your research questions or research purposes. In turn, research purposes may be broadly grouped into those which aim to:

1. gain familiarity with a given phenomenon and achieve new insights into its processes and dimensions often for purposes of formulating a more precise research problem or developing hypotheses. These are termed **exploratory studies.**

2. portray accurately the characteristics of a particular individual, situation or group, with or without some initial hypothesis on the nature of these characteristics; to determine the frequency with which something occurs, or the frequency with which something is associated with something, often with a specific initial hypothesis. These are termed **descriptive studies**. (PSSC : 2000 : 41-43). The types of descriptive research are **case studies, surveys, developmental studies, follow-up studies, documentary analysis, trend analysis, and co relational studies** (Sevilla, et al. 1992 : 96-110).

3. test a hypothesis of a causal relationship between variables. The information, insights and knowledge gained from exploratory and descriptive studies often form the basis for positing a hypothesis of a causal order or one which asserts that a particular characteristics or occurrence (x) is one of the determinants of another characteristics or occurrence (y). Studies which seek to test causal relationships often draw from the logic of experiments and attempt to approximate the design of **experimental studies**.

4. For the most part, the investigation of causal relationship / hypotheses in social science research is done through quasi-experimental designs. Quasi-experimental designs (QED) lack some features of the true experiment. QED may be characterized by:

    - absence of a control group,
    - the inability to randomize the selection and assignment of subjects into study conditions,
    - or the possibility of collecting measures only after but not before the experimental study (PSSC :2000 : 47).

There are three general types of research designs based on the purposes or intentions of the study:

1. The Deductive Mode of Research in a Quantitative Study (Figure 2).
2. The Inductive Mode of Research in a Qualitative Study (Figure 4).
3. Quantitative and Qualitative Study (Figure 6).

The Deductive Mode of Research

The deductive mode of research in a quantitative study is also called the Top-Down Model. At the top of the hierarchy is a theory which the researcher tests. Following the arrows downward, the research process is completed with the research findings. When the findings are in the hands of the researcher, he goes back to the theory at the top of the hierarchy and compares his findings against it. He then attempts to find out whether the findings confirm or negate the theory.

Researcher tests a theory

↓

Researcher tests hypotheses or research questions derived from the theory

↓

Researcher operationalizes concepts or variables derived from a theory

↓

Researcher uses an instrument to measure variables in the theory

↓

Researc findings

Fig 2. The Deductive Mode of Research

The survey method is an example of a quantitative research. A checklist of questions for designing a survey method is shown in Fig. 3.

________Is the purpose of a survey design stated?
________Are the reasons for choosing the design mentioned?
________Is the nature of the survey (cross-sectional vs longitudinal) identified?
________Are the population and size of the population mentioned?
________Will the population be stratified? If so, how?
________How many people will be in the sample? On what basis was this size chosen?
________What will be the procedure for sampling these individuals (c.g. random, nonrandom)?
________What instrument will be used in the survey? Who developed the instrument?
________What are the content areas addressed in the survey? The scales?
________What procedure will be used to pilot or field test the survey?
________What is the time line for administering the survey?
________What are the variables in the study?
________How do these variables cross-reference the research questions and items on the survey?
________What specific steps will be taken in data analysis to (a) analyze returns, (b) check for response bias, (c) conduct a descriptive analysis, (d) collapse items into scales (if needed), (e) check for reliability of scales (if needed), and (f) run mult1vanate statistics to answer the research questions

Fig. 3. A Checklist of Questions for Designing a Survey Method

The Inductive Mode of Research

The inductive mode of research in a qualitative study is also termed as the Bottom-up Model. At the bottom of the research process the researcher gathers information. Following the arrows upward, the researcher goes through the process of a qualitative research and ends up with developing a theory or a model. This is termed in qualitative research as theory or model building. The theory or model which you have developed now becomes your contribution to knowledge. This is what makes qualitative study seemingly difficult to pursue why researchers opt to undertake quantitative researches than qualitative ones.

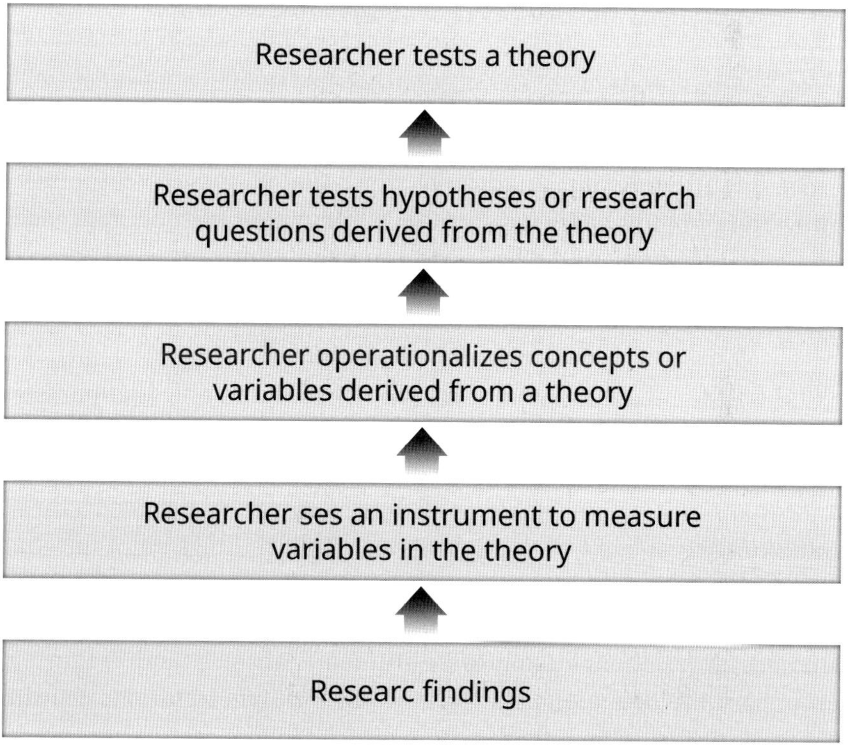

Fig 4. The Inductive Mode of Research

A compendium of data collection approaches in qualitative research is presented below (Fig.5)

- Gather observational notes by conducting an observation as a participant.
- Gather observational notes by conducting an observation as an observer .
- Conduct an unstructured, open-ended interview and take interview notes.
- Conduct an unstructured, open-ended interview, audiotape the interview, and transcribe the interview.
- Keep a journal during the research study.
- Have an informant keep a journal during the research study.
- Collect personal letters from informants.
- Analyze public documents (e. g., official memos, minutes, archival material).
- Examine autobiographies and biographies.
- Examine physical trace evidence (e.g., footprints in the sand).
- Videotape a social situation or an individual / group
- Examine photographs or video tap es.
- Have informants take photo graphs or video tapes.
- Collect sounds (e .g. , musical sounds, a child' s laughter, car hornshonking).

Fig. 5. A Compendium of Data Collection Approaches in Qualitative Research

The quantitative and qualitative study (Fig. 6) may be combined. This kind of study had been termed as the mixed method approach. According to Neto (2001), the mixed method approach is a research strategy integrating different methods. It is a way to come up with creative alternatives to traditional research methods.

Still on the mixed method of research, Cronholm and Hjalmarsson (2014) shared their experiences in their research using the mixed method. They analysed usage experiences from combining qualitative and quantitative approaches in different ways. They refer to these combinations as method configurations. Their findings point out that a researcher should commence with a qualitative approach when: 1) the researcher has a lower pre-knowledge of phenomenon to be studied, 2) the phenomenon to be studied is abstract and 3) there is an uncertainty if the questions asked are the right questions. On the contrary, there is a tendency in their results that the researcher should start with a quantitative study when 1) the researcher has a good pre-knowledge of the phenomenon or 2) the phenomenon is more concrete.

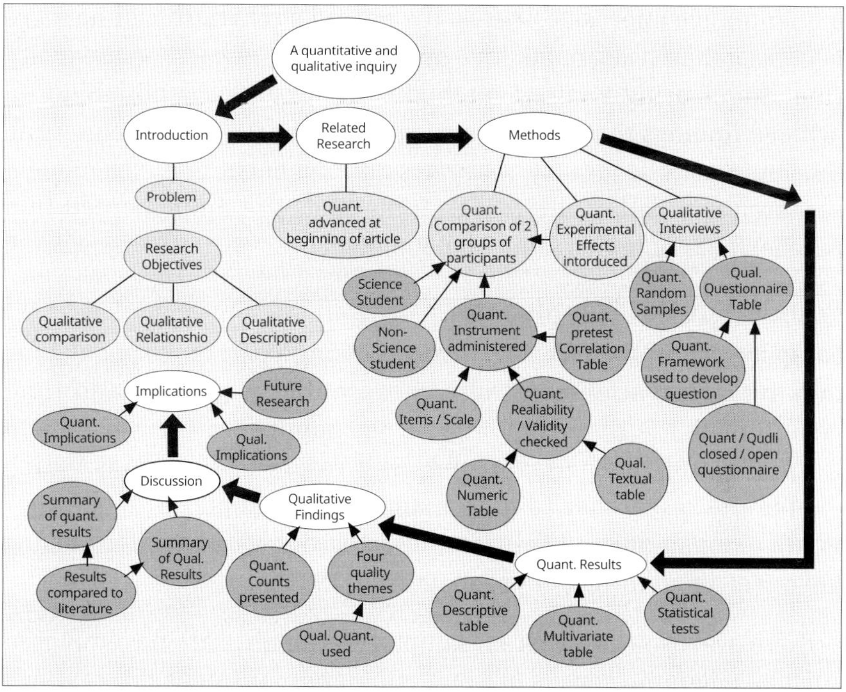

Figure 6. A concept map of the Quantitative and Qualitative Study by Gogolin and Swartz(1992)

Source: Data from "A Quantitative and Qualitative Inquiry into the Attitudes Toward Science of Non-Science College Students " by L.Gogolin F.S. Swartz, Journal of Research in Science Teaching, 29.

The aim of a quantitative approach is to suggest a hypothesis that should be verified or falsified while the aim of a qualitative approach is to generate a hypothesis. Simplified, it seems as the primary interest of the qualitative approaches is to justify "Is this the right question to ask?" while the quantitative approaches are more concerned with "Is this answer trustworthy?". Our view of research is that every approach has advantages and disadvantages. This is also valid for qualitative and quantitative approaches.

According to Creswell (2009) a mixed method is more than simply collecting and analysing data from a qualitative and quantitative approach. The mixed method approach provides a specific perspective of the world. Besides, it also incorporates a combined qualitative and a quantitative approach. That is, the overall strength should be more beneficial than using qualitative or quantitative research individually. One aim of using a mixed method is to increase the possibility to achieve findings that are more trustworthy and relevant than using the approaches separately. A key design component in mixed method research is whether the research methods are implemented in a parallel manner or in a sequential manner

Population and Sample Sizes

Sampling is the process which involves taking a part of the population, making observations on these representative groups, and then generalizing the findings to the bigger population (Ary, Jacob and Rozavich: 1981). The term sampling refers to strategies which enable the researcher to pick a sub-group (sample) from a larger group (population) and then use this subgroup as a basis for making judgment about the larger group (Vocrell: 1983).

There are instances wherein sampling techniques are not employed such as when the census of population and housing is taken which requires that all be counted. Also, when the population is not too big, the researcher may opt to do a complete enumeration.

When the population or larger group is too big and taking all of them would be unmanageable, it is wiser to get only a sample or a smaller group. This is where the use of sampling techniques is advisable. Sampling affords all the members of the population an equal chance of being selected and becoming a part of the samples of the intended research.

A common formula to derive the sample size was formulated by Slovin as follows:

$$n = \frac{N}{1 + Ne^2}$$

where:

n = sample size (smaller group)
N = population size (bigger group)
e = margin of error (the percentage of error allowed because you used only a sample and not the whole population. In the following example, .05 is the margin of error or 5 percent allowable error).

Gay (1976) gives some minimum acceptable sizes depending on the type of research employed:

1. Descriptive research – 10 percent of the population. For smaller population, 20 percent may be required.

2. Correlational research – 30 subjects

3. Ex-post facto or causal comparative research – 15 subjects per group. Some authorities believe that 30 per group should be considered minimum.

The different sampling techniques are herein described (Sevilla, et al: 1992:185-191).

1. **Random Sampling** is a method of selecting a sample size from a universe such that each member of the population has an equal chance of being included in the sample and all possible combinations of size have an equal chance of being selected as the sample. Because it gives every member of the population an equal chance to be a sample, this strategy is known as the best procedure. One example of this is the lottery sampling or fishbowl technique.

2. **Systematic Sampling** is a strategy for selecting the members of a sample that allows only chance and a "system" to determine membership in the sample. A "system" is a planned strategy for

selecting members after a starting point is selected at random, such as every fifth subject, or every tenth subject, etc.

3. **Cluster Sampling** occurs when you select the members of your sample in clusters rather than in using separate individuals. An intact group of similar characteristics is a cluster. This sampling is sometimes referred to as area sampling because it is frequently applied on a geographical basis. For example, a province which has three geographical areas will have three clusters, with every area becoming one cluster.

4. **Non-Random Sampling**. In non-random sampling, all the participants of the investigation are derived through equal chances. Certain parts in the overall group are deliberately not included in the selection of the representative sub-group. This is also called non-probability sampling or judgment sampling because it makes use of judgment in the selection of items to be put into the sub-group. Non-random sampling are of three kinds:

    4.1 **Purposive or deliberate sampling** – a criteria or purpose for selection become the basis for identifying the respondents. For instance, you want to conduct a tracer study of those who completed the training on cooperatives for a specific time frame. You want to follow them up after their training. So you do not get all the trainees but only those who finished training in 2011-2013.

    4.2 **Quota Sampling**. In quota sampling, you identify a set of important characteristics of a population and then select your desired samples in a non-random way. For example, you would like to know what percent of the community population use Colgate and Close-up as their toothpaste. You decide to study 20 percent of the 6,000 population. Twenty percent of 6,000 is 1200. So you go from respondent-to-respondent and ask them the toothpaste that they use until you complete the 1200 desired samples.

4.3 **Convenience Sampling** is a sampling strategy based on the convenience of the researcher. For example, you want to know who the most popular presidential candidate is. Just give your cell phone number and those willing to participate will just text back their choice and be counted in the survey.

5. **Multi-Stage Sampling.** This sampling strategy employs different types of sampling techniques. For instance, the scope of the study is too big, you may employ this strategy until you are able to narrow down the scope. The different stages may be as follows:

   Stage One. Cluster Sampling.

   Each regional division or area becomes a cluster. If there are three areas, then there will be three clusters. Get the total target population from the three clusters.

   Stage Two. Proportionate Sampling.

   From the population of the three clusters, determine the sample size. The bigger the population size, the bigger the sample size.

   Stage Three. Simple Random Sampling.

   After you have determined your sample size, do simple random sampling through the fishbowl technique. You can follow the procedure discussed earlier in this book.

Research Methods

Research methods refer to the methods or techniques for data collection and data analysis. These are not to be confused with research designs. A given research design can employ not just one but a combination or a variety of methods for collecting and analyzing data.

The more common methods for collecting data include:

1. The review of archival records and contemporary documents and others written as is usually done in historical research.

2. Direct observation of the phenomenon of interest, such as the direct observation of religious rituals in an ethnic community and the description and evaluation of these as is usually done in ethnographic research.
3. Participant observation wherein the investigator or researcher is also a member or participant of the group being studied.
4. Interviewing respondents about the research topic.

Other research methodologies for business research were given by *Dontigney* (2013). He stated that business research serves a number of purposes. Entrepreneurs use research to make decisions about whether or not to enter a particular business or to refine a business idea. Established businesses employ research to determine whether they can succeed in a new geographic region, assess competitors or select a marketing approach for a product. Businesses can choose between a variety of research methods to achieve these ends.He also cited specific types of business research methods such as case studies, surveys, interviews and focus groups. Each method is described below

Case Study. *When businesses want a comprehensive understanding of how customers interact and respond to a product or service, they conduct case studies. Case studies aim to develop a complete assessment of customer satisfaction, product use and attitudes about the product and do so in a relevant context. For example, a knife company might conduct a case study about its new, professional grade chef's knife by giving one to a professional chef to use for two months. Data gathering might include on-site observations of the chef using the knife, as well as an interview or survey. This method allows for in-depth information collection, but it is typically time-intensive.*

Surveys. *One of the more common research methods, a survey enables researchers to gather large amounts of data quickly and at a comparatively low cost. Due to the widespread use of surveys, a*

solid methodology and numerous samples make it fairly easy to put together a sound survey that gathers relevant data. Disadvantages of surveys include people in the target market not responding, partially completed surveys and shallow information about the target market.

Interviews. *Interviews often employ the same questions as those found on surveys, but they afford people the opportunity to respond at length. This approach typically yields deep information about one person's experience with a product, service or company. The opportunity to ask follow-up questions to more fully grasp a person's response is one of the key advantages to this research method. Interviews tend toward the time-intensive, and careless interviewers can bias interviewee answers.*

Focus Groups. *Focus groups typically consist of a small group of people consistent with a target market profile that discuss a product or service. Focus groups offer a kind of middle ground between other research methods. They provide a larger sample group than interviews or a case study, while taking advantage of the depth that interviews afford. As with interviews, however, the facilitator who directs the conversation can unintentionally skew answers in a particular direction, and analysis of the information collected during the focus group can prove difficult to analyze.*

Meta-Analysis. Insights on meta-analysis have been gathered by Sampa (2013). Meta-analysis as a research method has a widespread appeal in many disciplines. It is basically "an attempt to reduce the limitations of individual studies by trying to locate all the studies on a particular topic and then synthesize the results of these studies" (Fraenkel, J. R. & Wallen, N. E., 2008).

There are cases where the researcher through review of literature, studies, and other available sources finds that a researchable question exists on a persistent problem. There are evidently several studies that have been conducted on a phenomenon yet it seems inconclusive or unresolved over the years. The researcher may consider working on the findings and developing new conclusions based on re-analyzing such work, as in any other quantitative research, and aggregating them.

This presupposes that the topic still remains relevant and therefore the meta-analysis method is considered the most appropriate. In this way, the researcher may help avoid repetition but augment subjectivity in individual studies and facilitate consideration of the results of selected studies to get an overall index of outcome or relationships (Fraenkel & Wallen, 2008).

Some researchers have called this as "Secondary Analysis" or "Archival Data" because it entails a "social researcher not to gather his or her own data but to take advantage of the data sets previously collected or assembled by others" (Levine and Fox, 2000). The data may come from government offices, private agencies, and other organizations having a collection of data. It minimizes subjectivity, it is relatively quick and easy, and still exploits massive and even diverse data which is gathered in a scientifically sophisticated manner (Fraenkel, J. R. & Wallen, N. E., 2008; Levin, J. & Fox, J.A., 2000).

As in any method, there are limitations to meta-analysis. The researcher is limited to what is available and has no say as to how the central phenomenon/variables for example are defined and measured (Levin & Fox, 2000). Two other serious criticisms levelled against the method are that, "a poorly designed study counts as much as one that has been carefully designed and executed; and that the evaluation of the meaning of the final index remains a judgement call, although an informed one" (Fraenkel & Wallen, 2008).

To minimize the disadvantages and maximize the advantages of the method, the following measures may be taken. Limit selection and inclusion of sources to those that are closest to the topic under investigation. Consider integrating triangulation to inject bias neutralizers such as in-depth interviews with well-selected informants.

Storytelling with other purposively selected individuals can also help address gaps in data and reconcile emerging conflicts in some cases. Triangulation is one "of the most common analytical techniques to enhance credibility of a qualitative study. Such participants must be well-informed of the purpose of the study, the current state of the case, and no deception must be involved. Their participation should be voluntary and no risk must be involved in both the nature of information sought and the utilization of it. In this way the ethical criteria is assured (Creswell, 2008).

Meta-analysis is best in exploratory and descriptive qualitative studies. This means that the researcher is not confined to variables but pay attention to the emerging themes. This does not mean that the process becomes easy. It simply broadens the base and creates potential for depth because the research becomes exploratory and understanding oriented.

The purpose of Meta-analysis is typically general and broad focusing on narratives as presented. Collection of data is general and emerging forms may involve text or image data where a small number of individuals or sites are sufficient. As in other qualitative designs, analyzing and interpreting of data follows text analysis, description, and thematic development with the larger meaning of findings. Finally, reporting and evaluation is expected to be flexible, emerging, reflective, and biased (Creswell, 2008).

Instrumentation and Measurement

The Questionnaire. The questionnaire as a means for data gathering has oftentimes been referred to as the lazy man's way of gaining information. But as an inquiry device, it has gained widespread acceptance as a practical way of eliciting data for confirming or disconfirming a hypothesis. It has unique advantages and, properly constructed and administered, it may serve as a most appropriate and useful data-gathering device in a particular research project. It can be obtained directly or by mail (Manuel and Medel: 1985:56-57).

Here some general guidelines in questionnaire construction (PSSC: 2000):

1. Do not overload the questionnaire. Ask only the essentials. Do not make your respondents "data captive".
2. Make sure questions can be answered.
3. Make sure questions will be answered truthfully. Be explicit.
4. Make sure questions will be answered and not refused. Sensitive topics produce more refusals.

What to avoid in statement construction in questionnaires or scale items: (1) complexity, (2) technical terms, (3) ambiguity, (4) double-barrelled items, (5) negatives, (6) emotive language, (7) leading questions, (8) invasion of privacy: ad (9) organize items to avoid response sets of biases.

Guidelines for questionnaire wording:

1. include vocabulary that is simple, direct, and familiar to all respondents
2. be clear and specific
3. items should be as short as possible (20 words or less)
4. edit all items for readability

Steps in questionnaire construction:

1. decide what information to get
2. decide what type of questionnaire
3. write a first draft
4. re-examine and revise the questionnaire

5. pre-test the questionnaire
6. edit the questionnaire
7. specify procedures for its use

The Interview. The interview involves collection of data through direct verbal interaction between the interviewer and the respondent. The interview situation permits the researcher to adapt to the situation, working on follow-up leads, and obtaining more data and greater clarity. Its limitation lies in the bias, either eagerness or antagonism, that may arise between interviewer and respondent and may contribute to biased results (Manuel and Medel: 1985 :57).

The following procedures and guidelines are basically similar in all types of interviews (Metzler: 1989:15):

1. Define the purpose. Clarify with the aid of a written outline.
2. Conduct background research. This involves deciding on the topics to be covered to achieve the goal of the interview.
3. Request an interview appointment and be definite about time and place, topic purposes/goals and situations.
4. Plan the interview.

    4.1 Make arrangements to conduct the interview in a comfortable, private place to avoid distractions from other activities or interruptions from callers.

    4.2 Prepare yourself cognitively. Rehearse the interview schedule, knowledgeable in the practical aspects of the research subject. Orient yourself in the level, breadth and scope of language to use in the case.

    4.3 Affectively, have the right attitude. Practice taking respondent's points of view. Put yourself in his place and imagine your image/impression, approach, and vocabulary. Examine and discount your prejudices. Dispel ungrounded convictions, opinions, points of view or pre-conceptions and be authentic.

4.4 Physical, dress, appearance and social background should be perceived to be in common with the respondent to put him at ease.

5. Meet the respondents.

5.1 In breaking the ice, facilitate a flow of communication from the interviewee to the respondents.

5.2 Gain and deserve interviewee confidence for mutual confidence.

5.3 Establish pleasant association by a comfortable atmosphere, pleasant, courteous, neat and low-keyed appearance and attitude.

6. Ask your first question.

6.1 Begin with easy questions on pleasant topics.

6.2 Ask questions which will enable respondents to show and provide knowledge.

6.3 Adapt the following criteria in question writing.

7. Criteria in Question Writing.

7.1 Is the question related to the research problem and the research objective? The purpose of each question is to elicit information that can be used to test the hypotheses of the research.

7.2 Is the type of question appropriate? If you want to obtain reasons for behavior, intentions and attitudes, you should use open-ended questions, but if what you require of the respondent is a preferred choice of two or more alternatives, use a closed question.

7.3 Is the item clear and unambiguous? A statement permits or invites alternative interpretations and differing responses resulting from the alternative interpretations. Double-barrelled questions are ambiguous because they provide two more frames of references rather than only one.

7.4 Avoid leading questions.

7.5 The questions should not demand knowledge and delicate material that the respondent does not have.

7.6 The question should be loaded with social desirability.

8. Analysis of the Interview.

Interview notes need to be encoded and transcribed to an understandable and significant whole. Content analysis is done with a frequency analysis of a body of writing or speech. A good system of analysis exhausts all the potential information and provides meaningful breakdown for group contrast.

The Observation. The greatest asset of the observational technique is that it is possible to record behavior as it occurs and yields data that pertain directly to typical behavioral situations. Observation may serve a variety of research purposes. It may be used in an exploratory fashion to gain insights that will later be tested by other techniques; it may gather supplementary data that may qualify or help to interpret findings obtained by other techniques; or it may be used as the primary method of data collection in studies designed to provide accurate descriptions of situations or to test causal hypotheses. (Fonollera:1997)

As a research technique, observation must always be directed by a specific purpose. The planning for observation includes definition of specific activities or units of behavior to be observed, the nature of the groups to be observed, the scope of observation-individual or group, determination of the length of each observation period, and decision about the tools to be used in making the observation and recording.

You may consider the following factors in planning for observation (Good: 1986: 244).

a) An appropriate group of subjects to be observed.

b) Selection and arrangement of any special conditions for the group;

c) Length of each observation period and number of periods;

d) Physical position of the observer and possible effect on the subject or subjects;

e) Definition of specific activities or units of behavior to be observed;

f) Entry of frequencies or tallies in the record as a total for the entire observation period or by sub-division of time within the observation period;

g) Scope of observation;

h) Form of recording, including consideration of mechanical techniques and such quantitative factors as number, time, distance and spatial relationships;

i) Training of the observer in terms of expertness and

j) Interpreting observations.

REVIEW QUESTIONS

1. How do you differentiate research design from research methods?

2. Define exploratory studies, descriptive studies, and experimental studies.

3. When do we use quasi-experimental designs?

4. What are the different sampling techniques? Write a short discussion for each technique.

5. What are the guidelines for questionnaire construction?

6. Cite some guidelines for conducting an interview.

7. How do you compute the sample size of a particular research population?

8. What other research methodologies may be used for conducting business research?

MODULE 6

STATISTICAL TREATMENT OF DATA

FOCUS QUESTIONS:

After studying this instructional module the students are expected to answer the following questions:

1. What is the difference between descriptive statistics and inferential statistics?
2. What are the types of descriptive statistics?
3. How would you describe inferential statistics?
4. What are the different statistical tools to be used for specific types of researches?

Why Study of Statistics?

If you look through your university catalogue, says Lind, Marchal, and Wathen, you will find that statistics is required for many college programs. Why is this so? What are the difference in the statistics course taught in the engineering college, the Psychology or Sociology Departments in the Liberal Arts College, and the College of Business? The biggest difference is the examples used. The basic content is basically the same. In the College of Business we are interested in such things as profits, hours worked, and wages. Psychologists are interested in test scores, and engineers are interested in how many units are manufactured on a particular machine. However, all the three are interested in what is a typical value and how much variation there is in the data. There may also be a difference in the level of mathematics required. An engineering statistic course usually requires calculus. Statistics courses in colleges of business and education usually teach the course at a more applied level.

There are reasons why is statistics required in so many majors? The first reason is that numerical information is everywhere, in the newspapers, news magazines, business magazines, general interest magazines, or sports magazines (Lind et al, 2010). Here are some examples:

- The national average weekly income rose 2.5 percent, from $598 in 2013 to $613 in 2014. Inflation increased just over 0.1 percent during the same period.

- In 2014 the average U.S. household had $10,728 in credit card debt.

- A second reason for taking a statistics course is that statistical techniques are used to make decisions that affect our daily lives. That is, they affect our personal welfare. Here are few examples:

- Insurance companies use statistical analysis to set rates for home, automobile, life, and health insurance. Tables are available showing estimates that a 20-year-old female has 60.25 years of life remaining, an 87-year-old woman 4.56 years remaining, and a 50-year-old man 27.85 years remaining. Life insurance premiums are established based on these estimates of life expectancy

- Medical researchers study the cure rates for diseases using different drugs and different forms of treatment. For example, what is the effect of treating a certain type of knee injury surgical or with physical therapy? If you take aspirin each day, does that reduce your risk of a heart attack?

A third reason for taking a statistics course is that the knowledge of statistical methods will help you understand how decisions are made and give you a better understanding of how they affect you.

No matter what line of work you select, you will find yourself faced with decisions where an understanding of data analysis is helpful. In order to make informed decision, you will need to be able to:

1. Determine whether the existing information is adequate or additional information is required.
2. Gather additional information, if it is needed, in such a way that it does not provide misleading results.
3. Summarize the information in a useful and informative manner.
4. Analyse the available information.
5. Draw conclusions and make inferences while assessing the risk of an incorrect conclusion.

The statistical methods presented in the text will provide you with a framework for the decision-making process. In summary, there are at least three reasons for studying statistics: (1) data are everywhere, (2) statistical techniques are used to make many decisions that affect our lives, and (3) no matter what your career, you will make professional decisions that involve data. An understanding of statistical methods will help you make these decisions more effectively (Lind et al 2010).

Anybody in the process of conducting research, according to Manuel and Medel (1985), must be familiar with the language of statistics. Lind, et. al (2010) defined statistics as the science of collecting, organizing, presenting, analysing, and interpreting data to assist in making more effective decisions. There are two categories of statistics: the descriptive and the inferential statistics. Descriptive statistics is used to determine the characteristics of the data on hand. They tell about, describe, and define information. Inferential statistics go beyond the data on hand and extend to the universe from which data were drawn for the reader to estimate the characteristics of the sample. In general, inferential statistics can be applied only to probability samples, especially if it utilizes parametric tests.

Descriptive Statistics

1. Statistics of Location or Measures of Central Tendency

    1.1 Arithmetic mean. This is a computational average and is defined as the sum of the variables divided by the number of variables.

    1.2 Median. This represents the point on the scale or on the distribution where half of the variables is greater and the other half is lesser.

    1.3 Mode. The mode is the simplest of the measures of central tendency and is defined as the variable which occurs most frequently in a statistical series.

    1.4 Weighted average or mean. It is defined as the sum of the product of the frequency and the weight of a set of variables divided by the total number of frequencies. It is used for finding average of responses to opinions or items of the questionnaire which are given weights.

2. Statistics of Scale or Measures of Variability

   2.1 Range. This is the simplest measure of variation and is the distance between the largest and the smallest measurement.

   2.2 Standard Deviation. This is a measurement which shows how much the scores of a group deviate from the mean. Sometimes described as the root mean square, it is computed by extracting the square root of the sum of the squared deviation from the mean divided by n-1 elements when the sample is small, and by n when the sample is large. The greater the value of the standard deviation, the wider is the dispersion from the mean. A smaller SD means that the scores are heavily clustered close to the mean. A large SD would show that the characteristics of the distributions are heterogeneous while a small SD would reveal that the characteristics of the distributions are homogeneous.

Inferential Statistics

Inferential statistics deals with the description of the parameters based on the characteristics of a representative sample. Generally, in inferring the characteristics of the population frame, the samples utilized should be probability samples. Inferential statistics utilizes both parametric and non-parametric tests for significance. However, for parametric tests for significance, probability samples are desired. For distribution where normality is doubtful, non-parametric tests are used (Manuel and Medel: 1985).

1. Parametric Tests. Some of the most common parametric tests are the z, t, and the F-tests.

   1.1 z-test. The z test is generally used for testing significance when the number of elements involved in the problem is greater than 30.

1.2 t-test. This is used to test significant difference of the means of two independent samples. According to Broto (2003), the t-test is used to compare two means, the means of two independent samples or two independent groups and the means of correlated samples before and after the treatment. Ideally, the t-test is used when there are less than 30 samples, but some researchers use the t-test even if there are more than 30 samples.

1.3 F-test (Analysis of Variance or ANOVA). One-way ANOVA is used to test the significant difference of the means of three or more independent samples. It takes into account two sources of variations – from the between-group and from the within group.

1.4 Multiple Regression Analysis. The interpretation of the following values are considered important:

1.4.1 Multiple correlation coefficient

1.4.2 F-test

1.4.3 Partial correlation

1.4.4 The beta weight and its significance

1.4.5 The regression equation

It is recommended that the data be fed into a computer (Manuel and Medel:1985).

2. Non-Parametric Tests. Broto (2003) cites the characteristics of non-parametric tests. They do not require a normal distribution. Skewness and kurtosis are measures that give information whether the distribution is normal or abnormal. When the value of skewness is either positive or negative and the

kurtosis is greater or lesser than .265 the distribution is said to be abnormal. Non-parametric tests also utilize both nominal and ordinal data. Nominal data are expressed in categories while ordinal data are expressed in ranking. The most commonly used non-parametric tests are the chi-square test, Kruskal-Wallis test, and the Spearman Rank Order Coefficient of Correlation.

2.1 Chi-square Test (x2). The x2 test is a test of difference between the observed frequencies and expected frequencies.

2.2 Kruskal-Wallis Test or (H-test). This test is used to compare 3 or more independent groups. This is an alternative for the F-test (ANOVA) in parametric tests (Broto:2003).

2.3 Spearman Rank-Order Coefficient of Correlation(r_s). This test is used to find out if there is a significant relationship between two variables, the dependent and the independent variables (Broto: 2003).

A major problem encountered by researchers is how to select the most appropriate statistical treatment to suit specific studies. Often enough, they can do statistical computations but fails to choose the right statistics to use. In the succeeding discussion, Sprinthall (1994) presents some research simulations that clearly explains which statistical tests to use for what kind of research data.

Research Simulations: Choosing the Appropriate Statistical Test

Choosing the appropriate statistical test will depend on the kind of data involved in the study–whether that data involved are nominal, ordinal, or interval data.

Nominal or categorical data use numbers to label discrete, mutually exclusive categories; nose-counting data, which focuses on the frequency of occurrence within independent categories. An example of nominal data may be some kind of responses which the researcher may categorize.

Ordinal data are rank-ordered data that is, derived only from the order of the numbers, not the differences between them. Ordinal measures provide information regarding greater than or less than status, but not how much greater or less.

Interval data are measurements in which values are assigned such that both the order of the numbers and the intervals between numbers are known. Thus, interval data provide not only information regarding greater than or less than status, but also information as to how much greater or less than. Test scores are forms of interval data.

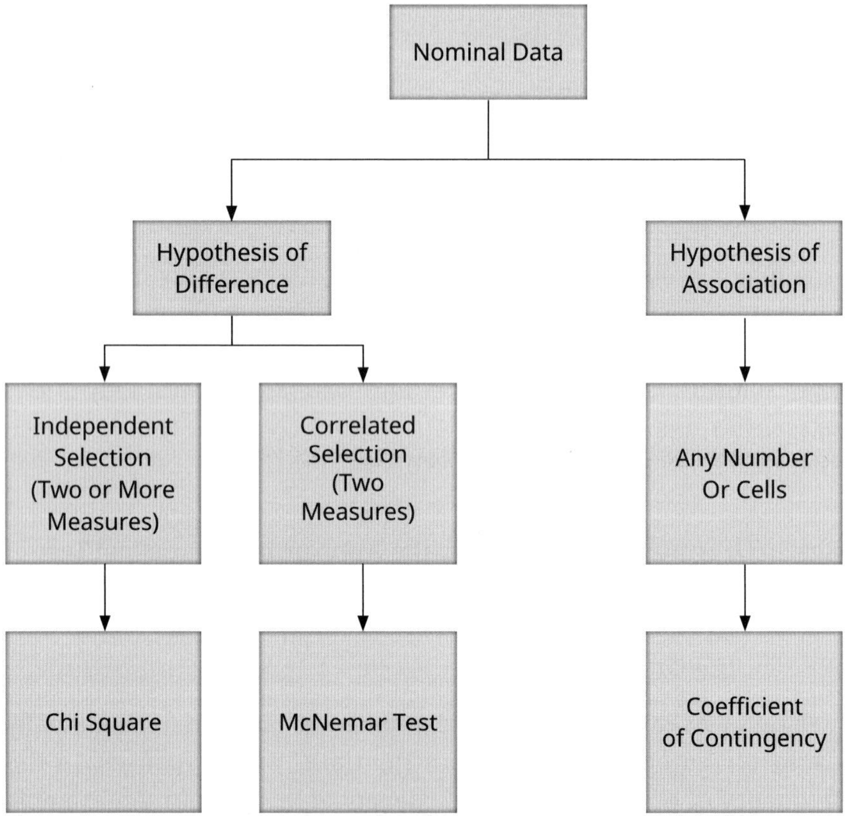

Figure 7 Nominal Data

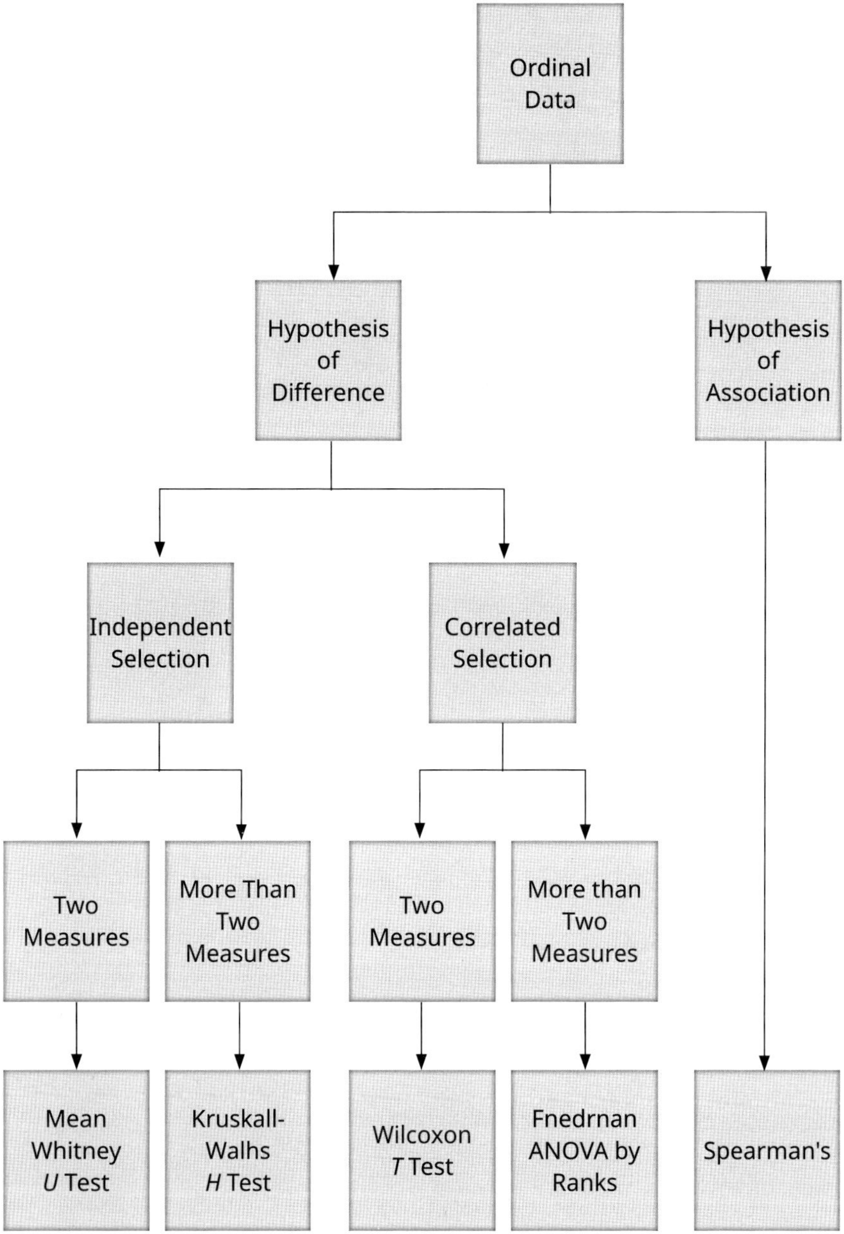

Figure 8 Ordinal Data

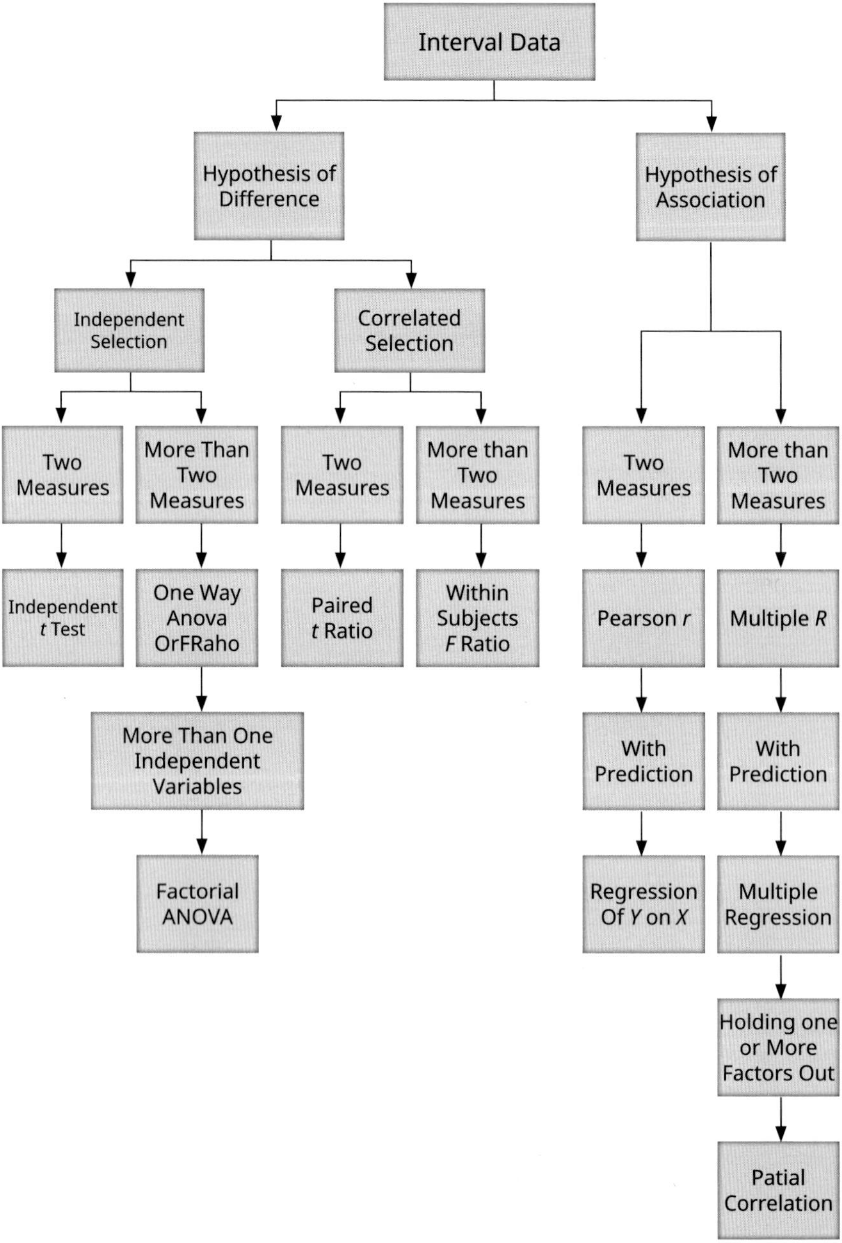

Figure 9 Interval Data

Research Simulation A

It has been traditional for the man rather than the woman to receive the check when a couple dine out. A researcher wondered whether this would still be true if the woman was clearly in charge, asking for the wine list, and so on. A large random sample of restaurants was selected. One couple was used in all restaurants, but in half, the man assumed the traditional in charge role, and in the other half, the woman was in charge. The data were in the form of the number of times the check was presented to each member of the couple.

Analyzing the Methodology. This is experimental research, the independent variable (man or woman in charge) was clearly manipulated. The dependent variable was whether the man or the woman received the check. Thus, if differences in the dependent variable occur here, they can be attributed to the action of the independent variable.

Answering the Checklist Questions: The Critical Decisions

1. *Scale of measurement*? The measurements of this study are in the form of nominal data - the responses being categorized on the basis of which member of the couple received the check. Use Figure 8.

2. *Hypothesis*? The hypothesis being tested is that of difference- whether or not a difference as to who received the check would occur as a function of who appeared to be in charge. (Since this was the experimental method, it had to test the hypothesis of difference).

3. *If the hypothesis of difference is tested, are the groups independent or correlated samples*?. The subjects (waiters or waitresses) were independently selected, since the restaurants were randomly chosen.

4. *How many sets of measurements*? There are two sets of nominal

measurements based on whether the man or the woman gets the check.

Solution. Use chi-square, in this instance a 2 x 2 chi-square, with the independent variable (who is in charge) in the rows and the dependent variable (who gets the check) in the columns.

	Woman gets check	Man gets check
Man in charge	a	b
Woman in charge	c	d

Research Simulation B

A researcher noting the positive correlation between socioeconomic status and amount of education, assumes there will be difference in the amount of TV viewing by the principal wage earners in high and low socio-economically placed families. A random sample of families is selected and categorized as having either high or low socioeconomic status on the basis of a number of measures (income of principal wage earners of all families were then contacted and asked for their hours per week of TV viewing. The hours per week for each socioeconomic class were compared.

Analyzing the Methodology. This is an example of post-facto research; the independent variable (socioeconomic status) is a subject variable, not manipulated. Regardless of whether the statistical test is significant, no definitive cause-and-effect statement can be made. Even if the upper-class group is shown to watch significantly less, the reason for this difference can only be suspected. (Perhaps upper-class persons read more, or work more hours, or have expensive time-consuming hobbies, or ... the list of possibilities is endless).

Answering the Checklist Questions: The Critical Decisions

1. *Scale of measurement*? The measurement here are in at least interval form. If one person watches TV for 25 hours and another

for 24, we know not only that one person spends more time watching TV, but also how much more time. With no evidence to the contrary, the distribution of number of hours spent watching TV is assumed to be normal. Use Fig. 10.

2. *Hypothesis*? The hypothesis tested is that of difference – that the two groups should differ as to the extent that they watched TV.

3. *If the hypothesis of difference is tested, are the groups independent or correlated samples*? The two groups in this case are independent of each other, each being randomly selected and then assigned to the high or low socioeconomic status.

4. *How many sets of measurements*? There are two sets of measurements, one for upper status and one for lower status.

Solution: Use the independent t test. Had it been predicted that one group watch mote TV than the other, then test as a one-tail t.

Research Simulation C

A researcher wished to test the hypothesis that taller men are more likely than shorter men to be judged as leaders. A random sample of 30-year-old men was selected and measured for height. The men were then brought before a panel of personnel managers and rank ordered on the basis of perceived leadership qualities. Each subject was assigned the median rank of the panel's decisions.

Analyzing the Methodology. This is a post-facto research. The independent variable (height) was not manipulated (although it could have been by using elevator shoes or even hidden stilts). Therefore, the issue of causation is not relevant here, although the probability of making accurate leadership predictions is very much at issue.

Answering the Checklist Questions: The Critical Decisions

1. *Scale of measurement*? Despite using the panel's consensus on ranking, the data are still in ordinal form. Although we may know that Subject 1 is perceived to be imbued with more of the leadership image than is Subject 2, we do not know how much more. Also, although height is clearly an interval measurement, it must be converted into ordinal rank before the statistical analysis can be completed (the men are simple rank ordered as to height). Use Fig. 9.

2. *Hypothesis*? The hypothesis being tested here is that of association. It is gratuitous to try and establish a difference between such already disparate measures as height and perceived leadership qualities.

3. *If the hypothesis of difference is tested, are the groups independent or correlated samples*? Not applicable; the hypothesis of association is being tested.

4. *How many sets of measurements*? There are two sets of measurements, height and measurement.

Solution. Use the Spearman's rank order correlation. Note that in this problem both age and sex were ruled out as variables, since only men of the same age were selected.

Research Simulation D

A researcher wished to test the hypothesis that older men sleep less than younger men do. Random samples of 30-year-old men, 50-year-old men, and 70-year-old men were selected. Each subject was brought to a sleep laboratory and measured as to how many hours of sleep per night occurred.

Analyzing the Methodology. This is a post-facto study, the independent variable (age) was a subject variable, not manipulated. (Age, can of course, never be a manipulated independent variable). Even if the results prove to be significant, great care must be taken in interpreting them. If it is found that the older men sleep less.. It may be they did so as young men, too. As youngsters, these men may have been more apt to rise early as a result of the differing cultural patterns that typified their younger days. This is actually cross-sectional research, the hazards of which have been pointed out).

Answering the Checklist Questions: The Critical Decisions

1. *Scale of measurements*? The dependent variable (hours of sleep) provides at least interval data, with an underlying distribution that is probably normal. Use Fig. 10.

2. *Hypothesis*? The hypothesis being tested is one of difference – that different age groups have different sleep habits.

3. If the hypothesis of difference is tested, are the groups independent or correlated samples? These sample groups are independent of one another. The fact that a given man is selected from the 30-year-old group has no bearing on who is being selected in the 50-to-70-year-old groups.

4. How many sets of measurements? There are three sets, one for each age group.

Solution. Use the one-ANOVA, the F ratio. If ***f*** proves to be significant, proceed with Tukey's

Research Simulation E

A researcher wanted to test the hypothesis that racial prejudice is a function of personal authoritarianism. A random sample of college students was selected and measured on the F scale, an index of personal rigidity and authoritarianism. All subjects were then given the A-S (for Anti-Semitic) scale, a measure of prejudice toward Jews.

Analyzing the Methodology. This is a post-facto study; the independent variable (authoritarianism) is a subject variable, not manipulated. Even if the hypothesis is validated, there will be no way to tell whether authoritarianism affects prejudice or prejudice affects authoritarianism. It is even possible that a third variable, such as a family's child-rearing practices produces both authoritarianism and prejudice.

Answering the Checklist Questions: The Critical Decisions

1. *Scale of measurement*? Both the F and the A-S scales are considered to be interval measures distributed normally in the population. Use Fig. 10.
2. *Hypothesis*? The hypothesis in this case is one of association. (One group is being measured on two different response dimensions). We can never test for differences between completely unrelated measures.
3. *If the hypothesis of difference is tested, are the groups independent or correlated samples*? Not applicable; the hypothesis of association is being tested.
4. *How many sets of measurements*? There are two sets, one for the F scale and one for the A-S scores.

Solution. Use the Pearson ***r***. If found to be significant, the ***r*** could be followed by a regression equation, with which specific A-S scores could be predicted from given F scores.

Research Simulation F

A researcher wished to increase the predictability of subject pilot scores on the FAA's written general aviation examination. Dependable relationships were found to exist between number of hours of ground school and FAA exam scores and also between IQ and exam scores. Finally, a small, but significant relationship was found to exist between IQ and number of hours of ground school. (Note that for the private pilot's license, the number of hours of ground school is not fixed by the FAA. A few student pilots put in many hours, and a few study on their own and never attend at all.)

Analyzing the Methodology. This is post-facto research. Although the pilots did experience different conditions (attending ground school or not), this was their choice, not the choice of the experimenter. Also, IQ can never be a manipulated variable. Thus, the two independent variables (ground school and IQ) were subject variables, not manipulated.

Answering the Checklist Questions: The Critical Decisions

1. *Scale of measurement*? The three measures (hours of ground school, IQ, and scores on the FAA exam) all yielded interval scores. The distributions all appear to be normal. Use Fig. 10.

2. *Hypothesis*? The researcher has attempted to test for associations among the three measures.

3. *If the hypothesis of difference is tested, are the groups independent or correlated samples*? Not applicable; the hypothesis of association is being tested.

4. *How many sets of measurements*? There are three sets – hours of ground school, FAA examination scores, and IQ.

Solution. Use the multiple *R*. The three separate values of the Pearson *r* (between ground school and the exam scores, between IQ and the exam scores, and between IQ and ground school) should all be used together to determine whether their combinations increase the predictive efficiency. If the value of the multiple *R* is larger than the separate correlations with the exam scores, solve the multiple regression equation. (Sprinthall: 1994)

REVIEW QUESTIONS

1. What is statistics? What are the reasons why the study of statistics is important?

   ____

   ____

2. What is descriptive statistics? Inferential statistics?

   ____

   ____

3. What are the types of descriptive statistics? Explain each type.

   ____

   ____

4. What are the different parametric tests? Non-parametric tests?

   ____

   ____

5. How do parametric tests differ from non-parametric tests?

   ____

   ____

6. What are the different statistical tests for research simulations A to E?

   Research Simulation A: _______________
   Research Simulation B: _______________
   Research Simulation C: _______________
   Research Simulation D: _______________
   Research Simulation E: _______________
   Research Simulation F: _______________

MODULE 7

PRESENTATION, ANALYSIS AND INTERPRETATION OF DATA

FOCUS QUESTIONS:

After studying this instructional module, the students are expected to answer the following questions:

1. What are the distinguishing features of the quantitative and qualitative researches?
2. How would you differentiate a textual and tabular presentation of data;
3. What are the three levels of interpretation? and
4. What are the guidelines in the presentation, analysis and interpretation of data?

PRESENTATION, ANALYSIS, AND INTERPRETATION OF DATA

There are two ways of of analyzing data. First is the **Qualitative analysis** which as the term implies, is not based on precise measurement and quantitative claims. Social analysis is frequently qualitative because the understanding of the phenomenon under study may not require quantification or because the phenomenon itself does not lend itself to precise measurement (PSSC: 2000: 51). Second is the **Quantitative analysis** which employs data that have been assigned some numerical value. Quantitative analysis can range from the examination of simple frequencies to the description of events or phenomenon using descriptive statistics, and to the investigation of correlation and causal hypothesis using various statistical tests (PSSC: 2000:51).

Saavedra (1997) gives some guidelines in the presentation, analysis and interpretation of data:

- The chapter is organized and divided into several main components or topics, each of which is titled according to the sub-problem or hypothesis statement.
- Present only relevant data. Individually scored raw data should not be reported in the text. If these need to be included at all, they should be placed in the appendix.
- In reporting data, choose the medium that will present them effectively. It will be helpful to summarize the results and analysis through tables or figures.
- Do not repeat the same data in several places and do not include tables with data that can be presented as well in a few sentences in the text.
- The textual presentation should supplement or expand the

contents of tables and charts, rather than duplicate them.

- Only objective data embodied in tables are made the bases of discussion. Highly opinionated and sweeping statements should be avoided.

- The analysis of the data should be objective and logical. Make a careful distinction between fact and opinion. Facts, not opinions, should prevail.

- In analyzing and interpreting data, point out those that are consistent or inconsistent with the theory presented in the study's theoretical framework. There are three levels of interpretation:

  a) based on inferences and deductions;

  b) based on documented evidences, supporting or contradicting the findings of the study;

  c) based on the researcher's insightful interpretation using implications and synthesis.

- In reporting statistical tests of significance, include information concerning the value of the test, the degree of freedom, the probability level, and the direction of the effect.

- The findings are compared and contrasted with that of other cited previous studies and interpretations are made thereof.

To have clearer understanding of how data is presented and analyzed in business research, a sample of market data analysis is presented by De Vault based on the work of Kotler (2003) and Lehmann, et. al (1997).

The market research process consists of six discrete stages or steps. They are as follows:

- Step 1 - Articulate the research problem and objectives

- Step 2 - Develop the overall research plan
- Step 3 – Collect the data or information
- Step 4 – Analyze the data or information
- Step 5 – Present or disseminate the findings
- Step 6 – Use the findings to make the decision

In the market research process, the fourth step is: Analyze the Data or Information.

The amount of data that can be collected and assembled in a market research study can be astronomical. Data organization and data reduction are two very important aspects of data analysis that is seldom highlighted. Yet, these steps are crucial to the ability to make sense out of data and to the ability to make cogent and insightful data interpretation. An impressive array of methods for data organization and data reduction are available.

A market researcher may tabulate data or compile frequency distributions. The means or averages and other measures of dispersion are common ways of analyzing data for which frequency distributions are available. Very often, advanced statistics and decision models are used to maximize the information that can be extracted from research data. The following section provides a brief description of several commonly used statistical tools, decision support models, and optimization routines

Kotler (2003) and Lehman, et. al(1997) described the quantitative market research decision support tools and how analyses is made using them. Examples are also given.

- **Multiple Regression** - This statistical procedure is used to estimate the equation with the *best fit* for explaining how the value of a dependent variable changes as the values of a number of independent variables shift. A simple market research example is the estimation of the best fit for advertising by looking at how sales revenue (the dependent variable) changes in relation to expenditures on advertising, placement of ads, and timing of ads.

- **Discriminant Analysis** - This statistical technique is used to for classification of people, products, or other tangibles into two or more categories. Market research can make use of discriminant analyses in a number of ways. One simple example is to distinguish what advertising channels are most effective for different types of products.

- **Factor Analysis** - This statistical method is used to determine which are the strongest underlying dimensions of a larger set of variables that are inter-correlated. Where many variables are correlated, factor analysis identifies which relations are strongest. A Using factor analysis, a market researcher who wants to know what combination of variables or factors are most appealing to a particular type of consumer can use factor analysis to reduce the data down to a few variables are most appealing to consumers.

- **Cluster Analysis** - This statistical procedure is used to separate objects into a specific number of groups that are mutually exclusive but that are also relatively homogeneous in constitution. This process is similar to what occurs in market segmentation where the market researcher is interested in the similarities that facilitate grouping consumers into segments and is also interested in the attributes that make the market segments distinct.

- **Conjoint Analysis** - This statistical method is used to unpack the preferences of consumers with regard to different marketing offers. Two dimensions are of interest to the market researcher in conjoint analysis: (1) The inferred **utility functions** of each attribute, and (2) the **relative importance** of the preferred attributes to the consumers.

- **Multidimensional Scaling** - This category represents a constellation of techniques used to produce perceptual maps of competing brands or products. For instance, in multidimensional scaling, brands are shown in a space of attributes in which distance between the brands represents dissimilarity. An example of multidimensional scaling in market research would show the manufacturers of single serving coffee in the form of "K-cups." The different K-cup brands would be arrayed in the multidimensional space by attributes such as strength of roast, number of flavored and specialty versions, distribution channels, and packaging options.

REVIEW QUESTIONS

1. Differentiate between quantitative analysis and qualitative analysis:

2. What are contained in the textual and tabular presentations?

3. What are the three levels of interpretation?

4. How are data analyzed and interpreted based on the different statistical tools used?

MODULE 8

SUMMARY, CONCLUSIONS, RECOMMENDATIONS

FOCUS QUESTIONS:

After studying this instructional module, the students are expected to answer the following questions:

1. What are the data and information contained in the summary of research findings?
2. What are conclusions and recommendations?
3. How would you write a summary, a conclusion, and recommendation?
4. Answer the review questions.

SUMMARY, CONCLUSIONS, RECOMMENDATIONS

The Summary

The summary presents in brief and very concise terms the following:

1. Restatement of the main problem and sub-problems;
2. Type of research methodology employed, nature and size of sampling groups of subjects or respondents and place of study;
3. Resume of the major findings which answer each sub-problem or hypothesis;
4. Findings are each stated in a statement or two, pointing out whether the null hypothesis have been rejected or confirmed and the sub-problems duly answered. (Saavedra: 1997)

Globio (2014) shared some guidelines in writing the summary of findings. The following should be the characteristics of the summary of findings:

1. There should be e brief statement about the main purpose of the study, the population or respondents, the period of the study, method of research used, the research instrument, and the sampling design. There should be no explanations made.
2. The findings may be lumped up all together but clarity demands that each specific question under the statement of the problem must be written first to be followed by the findings that would answer it. The specific questions should follow the order they are given under the statement of the problem.
3. The findings should be textual generalizations, that is, a summary of the important data consisting of text and numbers. Every statement of fact should consist of words, numbers, or

statistical measures woven into a meaningful statement. No deductions, nor inference, nor interpretation should be made otherwise it will only be duplicated in the conclusion. Only the important findings, the highlights of the data, should be included in the summary, especially those upon which the conclusions should be based. Findings are not explained nor elaborated upon anymore. They should be stated as concisely as possible.

SAMPLE SUMMARY

The sample summary was taken from the report prepared by University of Wisconsin Center for Cooperatives. The summary consists of the synthesis of the project purpose, project partners, data collection, methodology, and results.

- **Project Purpose**
    - The cooperative ownership model is used in a wide variety of contexts, ranging from the production and distribution of energy to delivery of home health care services for the elderly. Although cooperative businesses have been responsible for many market innovations and corrections of market imperfections, little is known about their impact as an economic sector. Until this project, no comprehensive set of national-level statistics had been complied about cooperative businesses, their importance to the economy, or their impact on the lives and businesses of citizens.
    - This report describes and quantifies the magnitude of economic activity accounted for by cooperative businesses. It describes the legal and economic characteristics that were used to define cooperative firms; methods used to measure cooperative activity across all sectors of the economy; and approaches developed to collect appropriate data. Finally, it provides a census of cooperatives, summarizes the extent of

their activity by economic sector, and measures their impact on aggregate income and employment.

- **Project Partners**
  - The project is funded by the Department of Agriculture with matching support from the National Cooperative Business Association and its members, and the Department of Agriculture, Trade, and Consumer Protection. In-kind support is provided by the Center for Cooperatives and the Departments of Agricultural and Applied Economics and Consumer Science.

- **Data Collection**
  - To estimate the impact of cooperatives, conducting a census of cooperatives was necessary. Cooperatives were located through lists maintained by trade associations, and academic colleagues; through web searches. In all, the study identified 29,284 cooperatives. Surveys using standardized survey instruments and a uniform sampling methodology, were then conducted to collect key business indicators from individual cooperatives. The surveys targeted firms in commercial sales and marketing, social and public services, financial services, and utilities. The study surveyed 16,151 cooperatives.

- **Methodology**
  - When businesses use capital, labor, and other inputs to create and sell a product or service, they create economic activity. The direct impact of this activity for the cooperatives in this study is measured by examining the revenue generated by selling output; income paid to owners and workers (wages, benefits, patronage refunds, and dividends); and number of jobs. The study used input-output analysis to examine how these direct economic impacts ripple through the economy to generate additional indirect and induced impacts. Conceptually, indirect impacts measure the ripple effect that

results from connections with other businesses: induced impacts measure spending by the cooperative's labor force and its owners with the wages and dividends (or "patronage refunds") they earn. The study uses IMPLAN, an input-output modeling system, to measure these secondary impacts.

- **Results**
  - Nearly 30,000 U.S. cooperatives operate at 73,000 places of business throughout the U.S. These cooperatives own >$3T in assets, and generate >$500B in revenue and >$25B in wages. Extrapolating from the sample to the entire population, the study estimates that cooperatives account for nearly $654B in revenue, >2M jobs, $75B in wages and benefits paid, and a total of $133.5B in value-added income.
  - Americans hold 350M memberships in cooperatives which generate nearly $79B in total impact from patronage refunds and dividends. Nearly 340M of these memberships are in consumer cooperatives.
  - Cooperative firms are fundamentally different from other forms of business organization. Assessment of economic impact solely in terms of the magnitude of business activity provides an incomplete perspective on the total impact of cooperatives. To initiate study on these more complex impacts, a series of eight discussion papers were p-repared. They address methodological and empirical approaches for exploring deeper issues on the economic and social significance of cooperatives, and, in part, will form the basis for subsequent phases of this research project.

The Conclusions

Conclusions are broad statements or generalizations that are based on the findings of the study. Broad generalizations not supported by data or findings should be avoided. Conclusions are logical, that is they flow from the findings. Implications are meanings not obviously expressed but could be deduced from the research findings.

Lee (2013) presents some insights on what conclusions are. She indicated that conclusions are logical deductions based on the data in the findings section. They usually include a comprehensive summary of the findings and ends with a statement which will lead to the recommendations section.

SAMPLE CONCLUSIONS

The decline in the use of the canteen was due to the following reasons:

1. Price and Quality of Food. While it was generally agreed that the price was reasonable and the variety wide, more than half of those surveyed felt that the quality of food could be improved upon, particularly in the areas of the taste of the food, size of food portions and freshness of ingredients.

2. Competition. Many canteen users, especially staff, were attracted by a new food court at the new neighbourhood shopping centre opposite the IT. Canteen takings were also affected by the six newly installed non-carbonated health drinks vending machines located in the canteen. Many staff also found sandwiches from the sandwich bar located outside. Compounding the problem could be that the canteen did not seem to serve enough types of healthy food.

3. Canteen Operating Hours. The respondents, majority of whom were staff, were dissatisfied with the canteen operating hours. They wished the canteen to be opened as early as 8 am to cater to those who wanted to have breakfast or avoid the lunch crowd.

4. Ambience of the Canteen. The ambience of the canteen was not conducive for having meals due to the lack of air-conditioning and high noise levels. The music played by the

newly installed juke box worsens the situation as the selection of music turns away the adults. Hence, to improve the canteen, recommendations must address the problems identified in the above areas.

The Recommendations

Further, Lee (2013) gives some insights related to the recommendations of a research work. She indicated that recommendations are logical and should flow logically from the conclusions; they are relevant and must meet the purpose and the scope as stated in the introduction section; they are feasible that they must be practical and workable.

Recommendations are suggestions for the improvement of practices, policies, and implementing strategies relative to the topic under study. The recommendations are divided into two parts:

1. specific recommendations on the findings and conclusions of the study itself; and
2. general recommendations

The specific recommendations are focused on the study's findings and conclusions. They envision how the findings can be used to further improve the pertinent aspects or variables that were subject of the investigation. The general recommendations point out suggested measures which concerned institutions and the government may undertake and implement for the betterment of society in general. Furthermore, the research recommendations should be based on findings. They should not be opinionated. Rather, they must be based on evidences.

Suggestions for further investigation in the same field may be made. Some closely related problems that seem to have grown out of the study may be mentioned. Modifications that may be introduced if one were to study the same problem again may also be given (Saavedra: 1997).

On how to write recommendations, Lee (2013) stated that they should be brief. They should be written concisely and that any reason for recommendation should only be given if necessary. Recommendations should be clear. Do not be ambiguous as to how the suggestion should be implemented. The should be precise because vague recommendations usually result from insufficient research/ analysis.

The following sample recommendations was prepared by Lee (2013).

SAMPLE RECOMMENDATIONS

To help increase usage of the canteen, the following recommendations are proposed:

1. Price and Quality of Food. To address the problems of size of food portions and freshness of ingredients, the Operations Department should encourage the canteen vendors to provide larger portions of food to customers. The canteen operators should also be told to use only fresh ingredients in their food. This could help to improve the taste of the food. Canteen operators should also look into improving the quality of their food by making weekly or fortnightly changes to the menus.

2. Competition. Canteen vendors can also try to add more healthy food and beverage to their menu like vegetable salads, sandwiches or health drinks. This can help to draw the crowd away from the new vending machines, sandwich bar and new food court.

3. Canteen Operating Hours. The canteen should begin operations at 8 am to cater to staff taking breakfast or early lunch. This new measure could be put on trial for one to two months before getting feedback from both staff and canteen vendors on whether the early starting time needs to be adjusted.

4. Ambience of the Canteen. To improve the ventilation system in

the canteen, fans should be installed. In the long run, plans to fully air-condition the food court can be considered. Students' timetables should be reviewed to allow for staggcrcd lunch hours between 11 am and 2pm so as to minimize the crowd during peak hours. This could also help to reduce the noise level during peak hours. The type of music installed in the juke box machine could be reviewed to ensure that it does not play jarring music that may turn staff off.

REVIEW QUESTIONS

What information are contained in the summary?

What are conclusions?

What are implications?

What should be included in the recommendations?

MODULE 9

DOCUMENTATION AND BIBLIOGRAPHY

FOCUS QUESTIONS:

After studying this instructional module, the students are expected to answer the following questions:

1. What is the American Psychological Association (APA) style of documentation?
2. How is the APA style used in documenting thesis and dissertation?
3. How is the Campbell, et al. style in documentation?
4. What are the different styles and mechanics used in research documentation?
5. How do you prepare bibliographical entries correctly?

DOCUMENTATION AND BIBLIOGRAPHY

AMERICAN PSYCHOLOGICAL ASSOCIATION (APA) STYLE

Although not a rigid rule, many schools prescribe the use of the APA style in writing. The decision to use APA style is a decision of individual schools. The APA style uses parenthetical documentation within the text. Instead of putting the author's last name and a page number in parenthesis, APA style places in parenthesis the author's last name and year of publication. Complete information about each source cited in the text are presented in the bibliography of the research report in alphabetical order (Fonollera, 1993).

The following are specific guidelines in using the APA style:

1. **Parenthetical reference citations in the text.** When you do not mention the author's name in your text, that name followed by a comma and the date of publication appears in parenthesis at the end of the sentence.

    Example:
    Organizational behavior is the study and application of knowledge about how people act within the organization (Cummings, 1989).

2. **Author cited in the text**. When the author is cited in the text, cite only the date of publication in parenthesis immediately after the author's name.

    Example:
    Cummings (1989) defines organizational behavior as the study and application of knowledge about how people act within the organization.

3. **Author and date cited in the text.** When the author and date are cited in the text, parenthetical documentation is not necessary.

4. **Sentence contains a quotation and name of author**. When a sentence contains a quotation and includes the name of the author, place the publication date and page number in parenthesis. Abbreviate page or pages (p. or pp.). The publication date should follow at the end of the quotation.

   Example:
   Cummings (1988) explained that "organizational behavior applies broadly to the behavior of people in all types of organizations, such as business, government, schools, and service organizations".

5. **Quotation without name of author**. When you quote but do not identify the author in the sentence, the name of the author, date of publication and page number appear in parenthesis at the end of the sentence.

   Example:
   The key elements in organizational behavior are people, structure, technology and the environments in which the organization operates (Cummings, 1988, p.5)

6. **Work by two authors**. When you refer to a work by two authors, cite both names each time the reference appears.

   Example:
   People also use technology to help get the job done, so there is an interaction of people, structure, and technology (Davis and Newstrom, 1989, p. 6)

7. **Work by two through five authors**. For a work by more than two authors, but fewer than six authors, cite all the names in the first reference. In subsequent references, cite only the name of the first author and use et al.

   Example:
   Selltiz, Jahoda and Deutsch (1981) said that research is a

wedding between theory and practice.

Selltiz, et al, (1981) emphasized the use of theory in developing the conceptual framework of a study.

The paradigm is a statement of the relation that a research wants to explore (Selltiz, et al., 1981)

8. **Work by more than six authors**. Give only the last name of the first author followed by et al., in the first and subsequent references.

9. **Authors with the same last name**. When you cite works by two or more authors with same last name, use initials to identify the authors in text even if their dates of publication differ.

   Example:
   J. Newstrom (1988) confirmed the findings of K. Newstrom (1977)

10. **No author and only title**. When a work is listed in the reference by title alone, a shortened version of the title is used to identify the work. The title of the book is underlined, the title of the article appears within quotation marks.

    Example:
    A triple rewards system is created when human, organization, and social objectives are met ("Human Behavior" **Management**, 1988)

11. **Corporate author**. When you cite a work by a corporate author, use the name of the organization as the author.

    Example:
    Graduate programs in educational administration are envisioned to train leaders (University of the Philippines, 1990)

    In subsequent parenthetical references of the same

institution, you may use abbreviations.

Example: (U.P., 1990)

12. **Reference to more than one work.** Parenthetical references may mention more than one work or multiple citations should be arranged as follows:

    1.2.1. List two or more works by the same author in the order of date of publication (Gould 197, 1989)

    1.2.2. Differentiate work by the same author and with the same publication date by adding an identifying letter to each date (Bloom, 1987a, 1987b). The letters also appear in the reference list where the works are alphabetized by title.

    1.2.3. List works by different authors in alphabetical order by last name and use semi-colon to separate the references (Gould, 1989); (Smith, 1983).

13. **A Sample Bibliography**

    Beer, Michael, Best Spector, Passl Laurence, (1988). **Managing Human Assets.** New York: McMillan Co.

    Dow, Eden (1987). **Pygmalion in Management**. Lexington, Massachusetts: Lexington Books.

FORM AND STYLE BY CAMPBELL, et al.

Other formats used in preparing research reports include form and style by Campbell, et al. (1982) This style is characterized by the use of footnotes and Latin abbreviations.

Campbell, et al (Fonollera, 1993) gives the following words of advice: "Accuracy and clarity in your prose are as essential as precision in your research. If your ideas and conclusions are to make a contribution to knowledge, you must communicate them to as large an audience as possible. Hence, you need to follow a conventional style and mechanics readily understood and widely accepted.

1. **Style and mechanics**. The style has something to do with your choices of sentence structure, diction, and tone. Since your audience is the academic community, your unity should be formal in diction and tone. The diction should be formal rather than colloquial. Contractions and abbreviations should be avoided and non-technical papers, numbers are usually spelled out. The tone of the paper should be serious, not ironic or flippant. Humorous, casual or conversational approaches are inappropriate.

   Most research papers should be written in the third person, that is, with nouns or third person pronouns (he, she, it , they). The use of first person (I, me, us, my, mine, ours) to call attention that a statement is your opinion has a weakening effect on the assertion by implying uncertainty. Tense is usually the present, but usually, it should be appropriate at the time of the events under discussion. The sentence structure should be active, forceful and varied, reinforcing your meaning. You may want to use compound or complex sentences and parallel constructions but be sure they are appropriate (Fonollera, 1993).

2. **Latin abbreviations**. Although Latin abbreviations for subsequent references are now rarely used, there are three common ones that are still used. These are *ibid, op cit.* and *loc. cit.*

   The abbreviation *Ibid.* (in the same place) is used in consecutive reference to the same source. If the second reference is to the same page as the initial reference, ibid. is used alone.

   When reference to the same work follows each other closely but not consecutively and when they refer to different pages in that work, op. cit. (in the work cited) may be used in place of the title and facts of publication. The author's surname without given name or initials unless another author with the same surname has been cited, must be repeated in order to identify the work cited. The name is followed by op cit.

For a second but not consecutive reference to the exact material (that is, the same volume and page) previously cited, substitute loc. cit. (in place cited) for op cit. The author's name, usually without given name or initial must appear to identify the work. Page numbers never follow op cit. and loc. cit. because they are unnecessary (Fonollera, 1993).

3. **Citation Taken from a Secondary Source** (Turabian, 1980). In citing the work of one author as found in that of another, both the work in which the reference was found (secondary source) and the title of the work mentioned therein must be given in the reference. In general, the style illustrated in footnote should be followed, but if it is more significant for the purposes of the paper to emphasize Hulbert's citing of the Jesuit Relations, the style of the second footnote should be used.

   [1] Jesuit Relations and Allied Documents. Vol. 59, no. 41, quoted in [or "cited by"] Archer Butler Hulbert. Portage Paths. (Cleveland Arthur H. Clark 1903), p. 181.

   [2] Archer Butler Hulbert. Portage Paths (Cleveland: Arthur H. Clark. 1903), p. 181 quoting (or "citing") Jesuit Relations and Allied Documents. Vol. 59 no. 41

4. **Articles in encyclopedias and dictionaries** (Turabian, 1980). In citing alphabetically arranged reference works such as encyclopedias and dictionaries, it is best to give the title of the article preceded by

   "S.V" (sub verbo, "under the word") rather than volume and page numbers, place of publication, publisher's name, and in certain cases the date, are omitted from citations of most reference works. The edition, unless it is the first, is normally mentioned.

But here just as word is in order concerning the policy of "continuous revision" under which the major encyclopedias have operated for some years. The number of the edition is not mentioned on their title pages, and the date of publication thus becomes the means of identification.

[1] Encyclopedia Britannica. 11th ed., S.V "Blake William," by J.W Comyers - Carr.

[2] Encyclopedia Americana. 1963 ed., S.V "Sitting Bull."

[3] Columbia Encyclopedia, 3rd ed., S.V "Cano, Juan Sebastian del."

[4]Webster's Geographical Dictionary, rev. ed. (1964) S.V "Dominican Republic."

5. **Sample footnote references and corresponding bibliographical entries** (Turabian, 1980). The following examples illustrate footnote and bibliographical forms exclusive of those used in citations of public documents and in scientific fields. The abbreviation "N" and "B" stand respectively for footnote entry and bibliographical entry.

Books

One author

N. [1]Paul Tillich, **Systematic Theology**, 3 vols. (Chicago: University of Chicago Press, 1951-63). 1: 9

B. Tillich, Paul. **Systematic Theology**. 3 vols. Chicago: University of Chicago Press, 1951-63.

Two authors

N. [2]Walter E. Houghton and G. Robert Stange, **Victorian Poetry and Poetics** (Cambridge: Harvard University Press, 1959), p. 27

B. Houghton, Walter E., and Stange, G. Robert. **Victorian Poetry and Poetics.** Cambridge: Harvard University Press, 1959.

Three authors

N. [3]Bernard R. Barelson, Paul F. Lazarsfeld, and William McPhee, **Voting** (Chicago: University of Chicago Press, 1954), pp. 93-95.

B. Barelson, Bernard R., Lazarsfeld, Paul F,; and McPhee, William. **Voting.** Chicago: University of Chicago Press, 1954.

More than three authors

N. [4]Jaroslav Pelikan et al., **Religion and the University.** York University Invitation Lecture Series (Toronto: University of Toronto Press, 1964), p. 109

B. Pelikan, Jaroslav; Ross, M.G.; Pollard, W.G.; Esendrath, M.N.; and Wittenberg, A. **Religion and the University.** York University Invitation Lecture Series. Toronto: University of Toronto Press, 1964.

No author given

N. [5] **The Lottery** (London: J. Watts, [1732]). Pp. 20-25

B. **The Lottery**. London: J. Watts, [1732]

No author given; name supplied

N. [6] [Henry K. Blank], **Art for Its Own Sake** (Chicago: Nonpareil Press, 1910), p. 8

B. [Blank, Henry K.] **Art for Its Own Sake**. Chicago: Nonpareil Press, 1910.

Pseudonymous author; real name supplied

N. [7]Elizabeth Cartright Penrose [Mrs. Markham], **A History of France** (London: John Murray, 1872), p. 9\

B. Penrose, Elizabeth Cartright [Mrs. Markham]. **A History of France.** London: John Murray, 1872.

Institution, association, or the like, as "author"

N. [8] Special Libraries Association, **Directory of Business and Financial Services** (New York: Special Libraries Association, 1963), p. 21

B. Special Libraries Association. **Directory of Business and Financial Services.** New York: Special Libraries Association, 1963.

Editor as "author"

N. [9] N.D Anderson, ed., **The World's Religions** (London: Inter-Varsity Fellowship, 1950), p. 143

B. Anderson, N.D., ed. **The World's Religions**. London: Inter-Varsity Fellowship, 1950.

Author's work translated by another

N. [10] Ivar Lissner. **The Living Past**, trans. J. Maxwell Brownjohn (New York: G.P. Putnam's Sons, 1957), p. 58

B. Lissner, Ivar. **The Living Past**. Translated by J. Maxwell Bronwjohn. New York: G.P. Putnam's Sons. 1957

Author's work contained in his collected works

N. [11] Samuel Taylor Coleridge. **The Complete Works of Samuel Taylor Coleridge.** Ed. W.G.T. Shedd, vol. 1: Aids to Reflection (New York: Harper & Bros., 1884), p. 18

B. Coleridge, Samuel Taylor. **The Complete Works of Samuel Taylor**

Coleridge. Edited by W.G.T. Shedd. Vol. 1: Aids to Reflection. New York: Harper & Bros., 1884.

Separately titled volume in a multivolume work with a general title and editor

N. [12] Gordon N. Ray, gen. Ed., **An Introduction to Literature**, 4 vols., (Boston: Houghton Mifflin Co., 1959), vol. 2: The Nature of Drama by Hubert Hefner, pp. 47-49

B. Ray, Gordon N., gen. Ed. **An Introduction to Literature,** 4vols. Boston: Houghton Mifflin Co., 1959 Vol. 2: The Nature of Drama by Hubert Hefner.

Separately titled volume in a multivolume work with a general title and one author

N. [13] Will Durant. **The Story of Civilization**, vol. 1: Our Oriental Heritage (New York: Simon & Schuster, 1942), p. 88

B. Durant, Will. **The Story of Civilization**, Vol. 1: Our Oriental Heritage. New York: Simon & Schuster, 1942.

Book in a series

N. [14] Verner W. Clapp. **The Future of the Research Library.** Phineas W. Windsor Series in Librarianship, no. 8 (Urban: University of Illinois Press, 1964), p. 92\

B. Clapp, Verner W. **The Future of the Research Library.** Phineas W. Windsor Series in Librarianship, no. 8 Urbana: University of Illinois Press, 1964.

Paperback series

N. [15] George F. Kennan. **American Diplomacy**. 1900-1950 (Chicago: University of Chicago Press, 1951: Phoenix Books, 1970), p. 48

B. Kennan, George F. **American Diplomacy**, 1900-1950. Chicago: University of Chicago Press, 1951. Phoenix Books, 1970.

Edition other than the first

N. [16] William R. Shepherd, **Historical Atlas**, 8th ed. (New York: Barnes & Noble, 1956), p. 62

B. Shepherd, William R. **Historical Atlas**, 8th ed. New York: Barnes & Noble, 1956.

If the edition were edited by someone other than the author, the edition number would be followed by the words "Edited by ________."

Reprint edition

For a work that has been reprinted, it is important to give publisher and date of the reprint following the usual information about the book as originally issued:

N. [17] Gunmar Myrdal. **Population: A Problem for Democracy** (Cambridge: Harvard University Press, 1940: reprint ed., Glouscester, Mass.: Peter Smith, 1956), p. 9

B. Myrdal, Gunmar. **Population: A Problem for Democracy**. Cambridge: Harvard University Press, 1940: reprint ed., Gloucester, Mass. Peter Smith, 1956.

Title within a title

A title of another work appearing within an underlined title is enclosed in double quotation marks:

N. [18] Arnold B Come. **An Introduction to Barth's "Dogmatics"** for Preachers (Philadelphia: Westminster Press, 1963), pp. 90-92

B. Come, Arnold B. **An Introduction to Barth's "Dogmatics"** for Preachers. Philadelphia: Westminster Press, 1963.

MODULE 10

GUIDELINES FOR WRITING THESIS PROPOSALS AND DISSERTATION PROTOCOLS

FOCUS QUESTIONS:

1.1 Before writing, take hold of the school's format for a thesis or dissertation. Every school has its own format to follow.

1.2 Conduct a comprehensive survey of conceptual and research literature. Your topic for a thesis or dissertation will determine which library to go to. In the Philippines for example, if your topic is in the field of social science (education, sociology, psychology, management, sciences, etc.) you can go to the UP Library at Diliman, Quezon City, the UST Library at Espana, Manila, The DLSU Library at Taft Avenue, Manila, the Philippine Social Science Council Library at Commonwealth Avenue, Quezon City. For topics related to agriculture, economics, etc. you can go to UP College at Los Banos, Laguna. The National Library at T.M Kalaw, Manila, particularly, has them all. For more recent developments in the field, you can do your research in the internet.

1.2.1 For conceptual or related literature, get the following information: author, title of article, title of book or publication, place of publication, publisher, date/year of publication and pages. These should be written on index cards together with the excerpts or text you intend to use.

1.2.2 For research literature or related studies, get the following information: author, title of study, whether it is a master's thesis or a dissertation, school graduated from, address of school, year graduated, whether published or unpublished, whether foreign or local and the pages.

1.2.3 What information to get from related studies: methodology, respondents, variables, research instruments used, statistical tools, major findings, conclusions and recommendations. The research abstract will give you all these information.

1.2.4 Study how to document from original sources and secondary sources. As much as possible, use original sources. Learn how to use ibid., op. cit., loc. cit. in documentation. The book of Kate Turabian on form and style will give you complete information on documentation.

1.2.5 Use updated references. For books, 10 years back is recommended while periodicals and journals should be 5 years back. The use of obsolete references is discouraged.

1.2.6 For the UEP Graduate School, the thesis format follows that of Campbell and Ballou and for the dissertation, the format used is that of the American Psychological Association (APA) or the journal style. You can refer to Kate Turabian's form and style for thesis and dissertation.

1.2.7 Most importantly, the tenses used in your thesis proposals or dissertation protocols are futuristic. It is only after you have conducted your study that you use the past tense.

CHAPTER ONE

INTRODUCTION

Background of the Study

1. Cite the reasons why you have chosen the topic of your study.

2. Cite the problematic situation which prompted you to conduct the study from the macro to micro levels, that is, globally, regionally, nationally and locally, to zero-in on the local setting of the study.

3. Support your discussion with legal basis relevant to your study.

4. Pertinent statistical data should support your claims.

5. Make your presentation emphatic and explosive. It should create an impact on the reader of your research. It should prod your reader to go on and find out what good is there in your research study.

Statement of the Problem

1. Make a general statement of the problem.

2. Cite the specific problems in logical and sequential order as they appear in your paradigm.

3. The problems must jibe with the paradigm, conceptual framework, hypothesis, methodology and research instrument.

Objectives of the Study

1. Write an introductory paragraph before listing the objectives.

2. The objectives should jibe with the problems. If there are six problems, there should also be six objectives.

3. While the problems are stated in question form, the objectives should be stated in the infinitive of the verb "to be." The objective should start with the word "to."

4. Do not be repetitive in the use of action words. You should vary them, say, for instance: to assess, to determine, to evaluate, to draw, to find out, etc.

5. The objectives should be stated in behavioral terms. It means that objectives should be SMART (specific, measurable, attainable, result-oriented, and time-bounded).

Importance of the Study

1. Name those who are to benefit from the study - people, institutions, agencies.

2. Cite how they will benefit from the findings of the research.

3. Do not fail to include the researchers as beneficiaries and what they are expected to benefit.

Scope and Limitations of the Study

1. Define the scope of your study, the parameters or boundaries of the investigation, the variables included and the respondents to be involved.

2. What weaknesses or limitations of the study do you anticipate? How are you going to handle them so that they do not become the bottlenecks of the investigation?

Theoretical Framework

1. Look for a core theory with which to anchor your study. The core theory should relate to your dependent variable/s.

2. Have other supporting theories. The supporting theories should

be related to your independent variables.

3. Your theoretical framework should be a well-knit presentation wherein which to hinge your study.

Conceptual Framework

1. Your conceptual framework should be hinged on your theoretical framework. The theories cited should be clearly explained and operationalized in this portion.

2. The paradigm, which is a schematic illustration of the conceptual framework should be discussed comprehensively to encompass the parameters of the investigation.

3. Describe how your variables will relate to each other.

4. The hypotheses to be tested should be clearly explained in this portion.

Paradigm

1. The paradigm should illustrate or concretize the conceptual framework.

2. The variables should be appropriately placed in their corresponding boxes. The use of one-headed or two-headed arrows will clarify which variables are to be correlated.

3. Write the figure number under the whole paradigm and label it.

Hypotheses

1. The null hypotheses should be clearly stated. Using the null hypotheses will aid in rejecting or accepting it.

2. The null hypotheses should jibe with the number of variables to be studied.

Definition of Terms

1. Key terms or phrases used in the study should be defined conceptually (conceptual definitions are taken from books, encyclopedias, periodicals, magazines and journals).
2. After the conceptual definition, define the key terms and phrases operationally or how these are taken to mean in your study.
3. Terms to be defined should be arranged alphabetically.

<u>CHAPTER TWO</u>

REVIEW OF RELATED LITERATURE

Related Literature

1. Make an introductory statement before you present your related literature.
2. Cite conceptual literature taken from books, periodicals, magazines.
3. The conceptual literature should be logically presented.
4. Statements copied from original sources should be typed single space/inset.
5. Long citations should be paraphrased. In this case, your should restate the author's thoughts in your own words.
6. Document your sources properly.

Related Studies

1. Write an introductory paragraph.
2. Arrange your research literature or related studies by variables.

The arrangement of variables should be based on the paradigm.

3. Cite those studies which are relevant to your study.
4. Present the related studies by citing the research methodologies used, the respondents, the statistical treatment, and the major findings.

Similarities and Differences of this Study and Those Reviewed

1. Cite first the similarities of the related study with your study. Then cite the aspects where they differ.
2. Cite the aspects that make your study original or novel.
3. Similarities and differences should be compared even to their minor details.
4. Have a last paragraph that would recapitulate the similarities and differences.

CHAPTER THREE

METHODOLOGY

Locale of the Study

1. Describe the locale or place of the study;
2. If your study is about the educational practices of a certain locality, present some educational statistics. If the topic is about health, present some health statistics and so on.
3. Include a map or a locator.

The Respondents

1. Describe your respondents; their characteristics and profile and

how you are going to identify them.

2. Present a table depicting your total respondents, the population and sample sizes, type, number, frequencies and percentages, and so on.

Sampling Procedure

1. Describe your sampling procedures; how you will derive the sample size, what sampling techniques will you use.
2. The sampling procedure should be scientific. Avoid arbitrariness.
3. Your sampling procedures and sample size determination should pass the test of representativeness.

The Variables

1. Describe all the variables and how they will be assessed or evaluated.
2. The presentation of the variables should follow the sequencing in the paradigm.

Research Design

1. Decide on what research design to use. Your decision should be based on the purpose of your research- will you do it to search a theory? To test a theory? Or to solve a problem?
2. Make a justification why you are going to use it, why you think it is appropriate, how you are going to do it, etc.
3. Cite authorities to support your choice of research design.

Research Instruments

1. Decide on the type of research instruments that will best gather

the data and information needed in your study. Will you use the questionnaire, opinionnaire, interview guide, observation? Will you use the triangulation method or a combination of other research methods?

2. From whom will you adopt your research instruments? Have they been validated? If so, are they reliable and valid? Is there still a need to revalidate them?

3. Do they possess the basic characteristics of a good research instrument?

4. How about measurement and scaling of these research instruments? Are they explicitly stated?

5. Make sure the instructions are clear and explicit. Erroneous instructions will affect the respondents' responses and likewise your data.

Validation of Research Instruments

1. Research instruments which have been adopted from previous studies usually do not need to be revalidated. But when changes or revisions have been made to suit the needs of your study, there is a need for you to revalidate them.

2. Researcher-made instruments need to be validated.

3. Decide on how you are going to validate your research instruments. Will you employ field testing? Expert validation? Or a combination of the validation techniques?

4. If you are going to frame your testing instruments, will you subject the test items to item analysis?

5. Cite your justification why you will no longer validate them.

6. Where will you validate your instruments? Who will be your

pretest group? How many will be involved, etc.?

Sampling Procedure

1. Cite the procedure for determining your sample size.
2. Decide on the sampling technique you are going to employ and why? Will you use a combination of different sampling techniques or procedures?
3. Make sure the determination of the samples and the identification of your respondents have been done following scientific procedures and not your arbitrary decision or subjective judgment.

Scoring and Interpretation of Data

1. Describe your scoring or point system for every variable. Your data quantification should help you in your statistical analysis.
2. Mention the source or author of the scoring pattern you have adopted.
3. Explain how your data will be scored and interpreted.

Data Gathering Procedure

1. Describe the step-by-step process in your data gathering, what you actually intend to do and the individuals who will act as research aid.
2. Take note of unusual events, occurrences, or comments of the respondents in the course of your data gathering.
3. If using the triangulation method, be extra observant of whatever that happens during the data gathering.

Statistical Treatment of Data

1. Describe the statistical tools you are going to use and for what purpose you are going to use them.

2. Indicate the different formulas and the legend for the symbols used.

3. Indicate also at what level of significance will the interpretations be based.

The Bibliography

1. The entries in the bibliography should be classified into four:

   A. Books

   B. Periodicals

   C. Unpublished materials

   D. Other sources

2. Books, dictionaries, encyclopedias, handbooks should fall under the first classification.

3. Newspapers, magazines, dailies fall under periodicals.

4. Related studies fall under unpublished materials.

5. Speeches, monographs, lectures, letters, etc. are classified under other sources.

6. The authors' surnames should be arranged alphabetically. (See Appendices for a sample bibliography)

Appendices

1. The following documents are placed under appendices: 1) Permission to conduct the study; 2) cover letter to respondents; 3) questionnaires, opinionnaires, interview schedule, observation guide, checklist, testing instruments, appendix tables, etc.

2. Make sure that whatever your append are related to your study and will be useful in facilitating the understanding of the text of your study.

GLOSSARY

Abstract is a summary of a study that describes its most important aspects, including major results and conclusions. (Sarno; 2010: 107).

Action research as defined by Fraenkel and Wallen (2010) refers to an activity conducted by one or more individuals or groups for the purpose of solving a problem or obtaining information in order to reform local practice. Ferrance (2000) defines action research as a process in which participants examine their own educational practice systematically and carefully using techniques of research. (Bondoc, et. al: 2014)

Applied research refers to the application of theory to the solution of problems. It is conducted for the purpose of applying, or testing theory, and evaluating its usefulness (Gay: 1976).

Assumption is any important fact presumed to be true but not actually verified. Unlike the hypothesis, it does not need testing or confirmation. (Sarno: 2010: 107)

Case study is an in-depth investigation of an individual, group, or institution to determine the variables and relationships among the variables, influencing the current behaviour or status of the subjects of the study. (Sarno: 2010: 107)

Cluster sampling is a kind of sampling in which groups, not individuals, are randomly selected. Any intact group of similar characteristics is a cluster. This sampling is sometimes referred to as area sampling because it is frequently applied on a geographical basis (Sevilla, et al. 1992:189).

Concept is an abstraction distilled out of the various number of facts that the senses perceive through observation and subsequently given a name. A concept is one's perception of reality to which is attached word labels. Different people hold different concepts of the same thing (Selltiz, p. 48).

Conceptual definition, also known as constitutive, is that which is given in dictionaries. It is the academic or universal meaning attributed to a word or group of words. Moreover, it is mostly abstract and formal in nature (Sevilla, et al. 1992: 27).

Conceptual framework consists of concepts and theories that explain what has been done and what has been said on the topic or problem being investigated. The theories cited in the theoretical framework are made operational in the conceptual framework.

Conceptual literature pertains to articles or books written by authorities giving their opinions, experiences, theories or ideas of what is good and bad, desirable and undesirable within the problem area (Sevilla, et al. 1992:53).

Conclusions are broad generalizations supported by data or findings (Saavedra: 1997).

Control variable is that variable controlled by the experimenter to cancel out or neutralize any effect of a variable on an observed phenomenon. (Fonollera:1993).

Convenience sampling is a sampling strategy based on the convenience of the researcher (Sevilla, et al. 1992: 191).

Correlation coefficient is a quantitative formulation of the relationship existing among two or more variables. A correlation is said to be positive when high scores on one variable associate with high scores on another variable, and low scores on the first variable associate with low scores on the second. A correlation is said to be negative when high scores on the first variable associate with low scores on the second and vice-versa. Correlation coefficients range in value from +1.00 to -1.00. Correlation coefficients falling near the zero point indicate no consistent relationship among the measured variables (Sprinthall: 1994: 489)

Correlational study attempts to determine whether a degree of relationship exists between two or more quantifiable variables (Fonollera 1993, p. 10). Correlational studies look for relationships between variables (Salkind:1997:223).

Data is an information about a sample. (Sarno: 2010)

Data analysis is the process of simplifying the data in order to make it comprehensible.(Sarno: 2010)

Definition means giving meaning to a concept. There are various ways of defining terms (Selltiz). One is by ostensive definition which is any process by which a person is taught to understand a word by using descriptions. The other one is by descriptive definition which is defining a term by using other concepts. Operational definition on the other hand, is defining a term by using a specific testing criteria.

Degrees of freedom. With interval (or ratio) data, degrees of freedom refer to the number of scores free to vary after certain restrictions have been placed on the data. In inferential statistics, the larger the size of the sample, the larger the number of degrees of freedom. With nominal data, the degrees of freedom depend, not on the size of the sample, but on the number of categories in which the observations are allocated. (Sprinthall: 1994: 489)

Dependent variable is that factor which is observed and measured to determine the effect of the independent variable. It is the response variable, the variable that appears, disappears, or varies as the experimenter introduces, removes or varies the independent variable. Dependent variable, also referred to as the criterion variable or effect, is the outcome of the study; the change or difference in groups which occurs as a result of manipulation of the independent variable (Sevilla, et al. 1992:138).

Descriptive research describe the current state of some phenomenon at the time of the study (Salkind:1997:210).

Descriptive statistics refer to techniques for describing and summarizing data in abbreviated, symbolic form; shorthand symbols for describing large amounts of data (Sprinthall: 1991: 489)

Distribution refers to the arrangement of measured scores in order of magnitude. Listing scores in distribution form allows the researcher to notice general trends more readily than with an unordered set of raw scores. A frequency distribution is a listing of each score achieved, together with the number of individuals receiving that score. When graphing frequency distributions, one usually indicates the scores on the horizontal axis (abscissa) and the frequency of occurrence on the vertical axis (ordinate.) Sprinthall: 1994: 490)

Documentary analysis involves gathering data by examining records and documents (Sevilla, et al. 1992:115).

Entry reference notes are techniques in note taking during the conduct of the survey of literature. The four types of entry reference notes are: 1) **Quotation** - the exact words of an author are reproduced and enclosed in quotation marks. It is important to copy each statement verbatim and to indicate the exact page reference so that quotations can be properly referenced in the written report; 2) **Paraphrase** - the researcher restates the author's thoughts in his or her own words; 3) **Summary** - the researcher states in condensed form the contents of the article; 4) **Evaluation** - the researcher records his or her reaction indicating agreement or disagreement or interpreting the point of view of the writer (PSSC: 2000, p 22).

Ethnographic research method is related to indigenous research methods in the sense that local conditions are involved. ERM is a method that deeply concerns being very near the people being researched. The kind of information to gather bears on the nature of information articulated by the subjects' behavior (Sevilla, et al. 1992:p 179).

Evaluation is the process of delineating, obtaining and providing useful information for judging decision alternatives. It is also the process of ascertaining the decision areas of concern, selecting appropriate information and collecting and analyzing information in order to report summary data useful to decision-makers in selecting among alternatives.(Fonollera: 1993). Evaluation is a type of research that determines why and how programs or services succeed or fail based on set objectives. It also provides basis for continuation, improvement or re-programming of specific project components (Tungpalan, 1997: 5).

Experimental control refers to efforts on the part of the researcher to remove the influence of any variable (other than the independent variable) which might affect performance on the dependent variable (Gay:1976).

Experimental method of research, says Travers (1978), is the most prestigious method of advancing scientific knowledge. Gay (1976) states that this is the only method of research which can truly test hypotheses concerning cause-and-effect relationship. Sevilla, et al. (1992: 138), states that in an experimental study, the researcher manipulates at least one independent variable, controls other relevant variables, and observes the effect on one or more dependent variables.

Expost-facto or post-facto research is a systematic empirical inquiry in which the scientist does not have direct control of independent variables because their manifestations have already occurred or because they are inherently not manipulable (Kerlinger:1973). It is that research in which the researcher attempts to determine the cause, or reason, for existing differences in the behavior or status of groups of individuals (Gay:1976).

External validity is the quality of an experimental design such that the results obtained are due to the manipulation of the independent variable (Salkind:1997:238).

Fact is that which actually exists, a truth known by actual experience or observation.**Field studies or cross-sectional surveys** may be used to examine associational or causal relationships between given factors or variables. They direct data collection and analysis on the different groups or situations that make up the study population and compare them in terms of the variables of interest in the study (PSSC: 2000: 47).

Follow-up study is employed to investigate the subsequent development of the participants after a specified treatment or condition (Sevilla, et al. 1992:115).

Format refers to the mechanical arrangement of words n the page indentation, margins, spacing, typeface, headings, page numbering and division of letter sections. (Egipto: 2011: 241).

Frequency distribution is a tabular method of showing all of the scores obtained by a group of individuals. (Sarno: 2010)

General reference are sources that researchers use to identify more specific references. (Sarno: 2010)

Historical research employs a cohesive, masterful style of narration of past events which aims at the critical search for the whole truth. In historical research, documents come as the chief primary sources of data (Sevilla, et al. 1992:91-92).

Hypotheses are testable propositions deduced from earlier studies or existing theory (PSSC: 2000:36).

Hypothesis is a proposition, condition, or principle which is assumed perhaps without belief, in order to draw its logical consequences and by this method to test its accord with facts which are known or may be determined. It provides guidance in the search of evidence, sensitizes the researcher to pertinent data and provides a unifying concept. (Fonollera: 1993)

Independent variable is one which is measured, manipulated or selected by the experimenter to determine its relationship to an observed phenomenon. It is the stimulus variable. (Fonollera: 1993) Independent variable, also referred to as the experimental variable, the cause, or the treatment, is that activity or characteristic believed to make a difference on the dependent variable (Sevilla, et al. 1992:138).

Inferential (predictive) statistics are techniques for using the measurement taken on samples to predict the characteristics of the population (Sprinthall:1994:492)

Indigenous research method questions the applicability and generalizability of western research methods. It recommends instruments prepared in the country. Response styles are locally oriented and data gathering structures are made consistent with Philippine reality (Sevilla, et al. 1992:179).

Informal interview are less structured form of interviews, usually conducted by qualitative researchers. They do not involve any specific type or sequence of questioning, but resemble more the give and take of a casual conversation. (Sarno: 2010)

Interval data are data which can be placed along a continuum or scale wherein distances between points are equal (Sevilla, et al. 1992:254).

Internal validity refers to the condition that observed differences on the dependent variable are a direct result of manipulation of the independent variable, not some other variable (Gay:1976).

Interpretation of research findings is based on inferences and deductions, on documented evidences, supporting or contradicting the findings, and involves the researcher's insightful interpretation using implications and synthesis (Saavedra:1997).

Interview or oral questionnaire involves a face-to-face question and answer session between the interviewer and interviewee/s to gather facts and information relative to certain issues (PSSC:2000:214). Interview generally refers to acts of communication which one person requests for information and the other person supplies it. Specifically, it refers to a specialized pattern of verbal interaction initiated for a specific purpose and focused on some specific content area, with subsequent elimination of extraneous materials (Garden, 1972).

Jargon is a word peculiar to a particular activity or profession. (Egipto: 2011: 242).

Level of significance refers to the probability that discrepancy between a sample statistic and a specified population parameter is due to sample error or chance. Commonly used significance levels in educational research are .05 and .01 (Sarno: 2010)

Likert scale is a self-reporting scale instrument in which an individual responds to a series of statements by indicating the extent of agreement. Each choice is given a numerical value and the total score is presumed to indicate the attitude or belief in question. (Sarno: 2010)

Limitation is a phase or aspect of the investigation which may affect the result adversely but over which the researcher has no control (Sevilla, et al. 1992:19).

Literature review is the systematic identification, location, and analysis of documents containing information related to a research problem.(Sarno: 2010)-

Mixed-method approach is a research strategy integrating different methods. The mixed method is a way to come up with creative alternatives to traditional or more monolithic ways to conceive and implement evaluation (Neto: 2001).

Moderate variable is a special type of independent variable, a secondary independent variable. It is the factor which is measured, manipulated or selected by the experimenter to discover whether it modifies the relationship of the independent variable to an observed phenomenon.(Fonollera:1993).

Multiple correlation is a numerical index describing the relationship between predicted and actual scores using multiple regression. (Sarno: 2010)

Multiple regression. Technique using the multiple R for making predictions of one variable given measures on two or more others (Sprinthall: 1994:493)

Multivariate relationships are descriptive studies where two or more variables are looked into in relation to other variables (Fonollera, 1993, p. 10).

Nominal data are used to label or categorize observations and which do not have any greater than or less than relations to each other (Sevilla, et al. 1992:37).

Null hypotheses are testable propositions which point the absence of a relationship among the variables (PSSC:2000:37).

Observation is the process in which one or more persons observe what is occurring in some real-life situations, and they classify and record pertinent happenings according to some planned scheme. It is used to evaluate the overt behavior of individuals in controlled and uncontrolled situations. (Fonollera:1993).

Operational definition is also known as the functional definition. Operational definition may be measured and experimental. The measured operational definition states the way the concept is measured in the investigation. In an experimental operational definition, the researcher may spell out the details of the manipulation of a variable (Sevilla, et al. 1992: 27-28).

Ordinal data are rank-ordered data with respect to a trait or achievement or performance. As such, ordinal data are characterized by greater than, equal to and less than relations (Kerlinger:1973).

Participant observation refers to a situation where the investigator or observer is also a member or a participant of the group/collectivity that he or she is studying. (Fonollera: 1993)

Participatory research method refers to a kind of investigation that starts with the definition of a problem by people who feel and think that it is a problem. It is the people themselves who develop their own theories and solutions to the problem. How they will go about solving the problem will depend on how they perceive it themselves and on their resources which are available to enable them to solve it (Sevilla, et al. 1992: 179).

Population refers to the group to which the researcher would like the results of a study to be generalizable; it includes all individuals with specific characteristics. Sarno: 2010)

Prewriting is a stage in writing where the writer records his thoughts quickly. He lists down all possible relevant, accurate facts thatare related to the purpose of writing. (Egipto: 2011: 245).

Problem is a perceived difficulty, a recognition of some discordance, a feeling of discomfort over lack of understanding or explanation for a given phenomenon (PSSC: 2001:27).

Pure research or basic research is conducted primarily to test or arrive at a theory. Its main objective is to establish general principles without known or intended practical applicability of the findings. It is in search of knowledge for knowledge's sake (Fox: 1969).

Purposive sampling or deliberate sampling refers to the selection or identification of research respondents based on a specific purpose using a criteria for selection. (Fonollera: 1993).

Qualitative mode of research is not based on precise measurement and quantitative claims. Social analysis is frequently qualitative because the understanding of the phenomenon under study may not require quantification or the phenomenon itself does not lend itself to precise measurement (PSSC:2000:51).

Quantitative mode of research is employed on data that have been assigned numerical value. Quantitative analysis can range from the examination of simple frequencies/frequency distributions, to the description of events or phenomenon using descriptive statistics, and to the investigation of correlation and causal hypotheses using various statistical tests (PSSC: 2000: 51).

Quasi-experimental design is one method of experimental research which lack some features of the true experiment. Quasi-experimental studies may be characterized by the absence of a control group, the inability to randomize the selection and assignment of subjects into study conditions, or the possibility of collecting measures such as in "after-only designs" (PSSC: 1992: 47).

Questionnaire, a tool for research, contains a list of questions which the respondents are requested to respond to. The questions which are standardized may either be the closed form or the open form. The questions in the closed form permit only certain responses, while those in the open form show the respondents to make any responses they wish to make in their own words (Sevilla, et al 1992:231). Questionnaire is a form prepared and distributed to secure responses or facts to certain questions, information about conditions or practices of which the respondent is presumed to have knowledge. A major instrument for data gathering in descriptive studies, it is used to inquire into the opinions and attitudes of a group and to secure information from varied and widely scattered sources, as well as from any range or territory, sometimes national or international. The questionnaire is very useful when time and place do not allow the researcher to see all the respondents personally.

Reality is the "what is" in the vast phenomenon called the universe, thought of as empirically verifiable, and can be perceived through the senses. (Fonollera: 1993).

Random sampling is a method of selecting a sample size from a universe such that each member of the population has an equal chance of being included in the sample (Weirsman: 1975).

Recommendations are suggestions based on the findings of a study. They envision how the findings can be used to further improve the pertinent aspects or variables that were the subject of the investigation (Saavedra:1997).

Related studies refer to researches which have been conducted and which have bearing on the topic under investigation.

Reliability refer to the degree of consistency, precision or accuracy that a measuring instrument demonstrates (Sevilla, et al. 1992:196).

Research means searching for a theory, for testing theory, or for solving a problem (Sevilla, et al. 1992: 25).

Research design refers to the strategy to integrate the different components of the research project in a cohesive and coherent way (Neto: 2001).

Research diffusion refers to the strategies for the dissemination of research results such as through videos, slides, tape recordings, radio, press release, comics, cartoons, research seminars, and creative forms such as puppetry, songs, poems (Tungpalan:1997).

Research literature refers to published or unpublished reports of actual research studies done previously (Sevilla, et al. 1992:53).

Respondents refer to individuals involved in a study from whose responses data are derived.

Review of Related Literature is an aspect of the research process which involves the systematic identification, location, and analysis of documents containing information related to the research problem (Sevilla, et al. 1992:52).

Scientific Law is a summary of available knowledge of the relationship between properties in more general terms than the empirical findings on which it is based. Scientific laws are hypotheses considered to be true (Kerlinger, p. 11).

Sample is the small group that is observed; any sub-aggregate drawn from the population (Ferguson: 1974).

Sampling is the process which involves taking a part of a population, making observations on this representative group and then generalizing the findings to the bigger population (Sevilla, et al. 1992:192).

Scientific research refers to the systematic, controlled, empirical, and critical investigation of hypothetical propositions about the presumed relations among natural phenomenon (Kerlinger: 1973).

Scope of the investigation defines where and when the study was conducted and who the subjects were. The scope sets the delimitations and establishes the boundaries of the study (Sevilla, et al. 1992: 27).

Social science research is the systematic observation, documentation and analysis of social phenomena. It entails the measurement, classification, analysis and interpretation of social facts for the purpose of understanding underlying trends and patterns in social phenomena, as well as their causes and consequences. It also aims to arrive at generalizations based on the empirical observation of social phenomena and formulate theories that help explain various aspects of social life, relationship and functioning (PSSC: 2000: 2).

Stratified sampling is defined as a strategy for selecting samples in such a way that specific sub-groups (strata) will have a sufficient number of representatives within the sample to provide sample numbers for sub-analysis of the members of these sub-groups (Vockell: 1983).

Surveys are studies employed to measure the existing phenomenon without inquiring into why it exists. The main intention is to use the data for problem solving rather than for hypotheses testing (Sevilla, et al. 1992:99).

Systematic sampling is a strategy for selecting the members of a sample that allows only chance and a "system" to determine membership in a sample (Sevilla, et al. 1992: 187).

Theoretical framework indicates all the constructs (concepts), definitions and propositions that relate to a research problem. It is an organized body that explains what has been done and what has been said on the topic or problem being investigated (Sevilla, et al. 1992: 64).

Theory is a set of interrelated constructs (concepts), definitions, and propositions that presents a systematic view of phenomena by specifying relations among variables, with the purpose of explaining and predicting the phenomena (Sevilla, et al. 1992: 45).

Trend analysis involves studies that seek future status. Its is employed in studies which aim to project the demands or needs of the people in the future (Sevilla, et al. 1992: 115).

Triangulation method tests the consistency of findings obtained through different instruments such as the questionnaire, interview, and observations (Sevilla, et al. 1992: 115).

Variable is a characteristic that has two or more actually exclusive values or properties. Variables are the construct or properties being studied (Sevilla, et al. 1992: 28). Variables are conceived and picked out from the theoretical framework. The variables are the categories of concepts of the research paradigm. They are plain information. The selection and control of the variables entail a rigorous process. (Fonollera: 1993).

APPENDIX A

FORMAT FOR THESIS AND DISSERTATION

This is a sample format for theses and dissertation prescribed in the University of Eastern Philippines, University Town, Northern Samar. Other schools prescribe different formats

TABLE OF CONTENTS

APPENDIX B

NATIONAL HIGHER EDUCATION RESEARCH AGENDA

Priority Research Areas

The National Higher Education Research Agenda (NHERA) integrates the concerns of the higher education sector with the overall development goals and objectives of the country and the higher education international community. The present priorities are as follows:

Higher Education Cluster	Research Areas
1. Science and Mathematics	Multidisciplinary research aimed to advance the frontiers of science and mathematics Leading-edge scientific research Use of scientific principles in responding to the development needs of the country Breakthrough or pioneering researches
2. Engineering, Maritime Studies, and Architecture	Multidisciplinary research on the improvement of engineering designs and concepts Engineering research with social and economic impact Leading-edge in technological research Breakthrough or pioneering research
3. Humanities, Social Science and Communication	Multidisciplinary research on Philippine Literature Peace and development studies with direct application to Philippine situations Policy-oriented research on HUSOCOM

4. Agriculture and Fisheries	Multidisciplinary research on agriculture and Philippine economy Use of scientific principles to enhance fisheries and agricultural productivity Breakthrough or pioneering researches
5. Business and Industry	Policy-oriented researches leading to improvements in Philippine business and economic sectors Multidisciplinary research on Philippines economics, industry, and business
6. Health and Health-Related Discipline	Multidisciplinary research on health and health-related disciplines leading to better quality of life for Filipinos; and the delivery of basic health services to the rural areas Policy-oriented health researches
7. Information and Technology	Policy researches on information and technology Technological researches for the advancement of Philippine Information and technology
8. Teacher Education	Policy-oriented researches focused on quality and excellence, relevance and responsiveness and equity in higher education Technological inputs to teacher education
9. Industrial Technology	Policy-researches on industrial technology Researches on product development Researches on enterprise incubation
10. Across Higher Education Emphases	Program/Curricular Assessment Researches on Integrative Theories, Models, or Philosophy Studies on Financing Higher Education Studies on Governance Studies on Accreditation Model Building Studies Institution-Building Studies Manpower Supply and Demand Integrative Studies in Linguistics, Sociology, Anthropology, the Social Sciences and Humanities.

APPENDIX C

SAMPLE INDEX CARD ENTRIES

(Related Literature)

Hilgard, Ernest T. (1995)

An Introduction to Psychology

6th edition

US: Harcourt Brace Jovanovich

pp. 265-66

Emotional attitudes and anxieties can have profound effect on our learning efficiency. Personal problems unrelated to the learning situation may interfere with concentration and sap the energy required for effective study. A certain level of anxiety may facilitate performance by increasing motivation, but excessive concern over grades and tests may be self-defeating. Although no one can deny that grades are important in these days of specialization, the student who studies because he wants to widen his fund of information will be less anxious in a test situation than one whose sole concern in an extrinsic reward, test grade. The former has achieved something of value and has progressed regardless of the test grade; the latter feels that his effort have been wasted if he does not get the desired grade.

APPENDIX D

SAMPLE INDEX CARD ENTRIES
(Related Studies)

Tolentino, Regina R.

"Stress Management Strategies Among Notre Dame Faculty and Administrators"

Unpublished Master's Thesis, Notre Dame University

Cotabato City, 2000.

The study made use of the descriptive design because it describes the characteristics of the respondents and their assessment of stress management strategies in terms of their stressors, manifestations of job related stress and problems related to these. The summary of findings are: (1) On the stressors experience, the faculty and administrators answered rarely manifested symptoms as indicated by the overall mean; (3) The faculty and administrators practice stress management oftentimes; (4) Problems related to stress management to which the faculty and administrators were asked to respond to were perceived by them as slightly a problem; and (5) Stress can affect both male and female at any given situation.

APPENDIX E

SAMPLE THEORETICAL FRAMEWORK

FOCUS QUESTIONS:

To provide anchor and support for the present investigation, the following theories are cited:

Maslow's categorization of human needs may prove useful in explaining what motivates individuals to become members of groups involved in issues of community change. He postulated five levels of needs and indicated that if these needs at the various levels are not satisfied, they remain very strong influence on motivation.

At the lowest level but pre-eminent in importance are the needs for physical survival. The rewards for group action in pursuit of gratification of these needs must be extrinsic and concrete, or the individual will abandon collective action. The type of project and the benefits they will receive therefore allude to this theory's need level. Material and social benefits seem to be the most popular and evident kind of rewards derived from a particular kind of project which will spell the difference in their participation in self-help projects.

On the second level are the safety needs – the wish for protection against danger, threat and deprivation. In modern society, these needs will be particularly felt if the individuals feel that they are the object of arbitrary authority or in a dependent relationship. They are likely to find gratification in a collectivity whose norm is interdependence and whose goal is to ensure the rights of the powerless and the underprivileged. Thus, the person's membership in organizations relate to their participation. When they are secured due to their organizational affiliation, the better would be their participation.

On the next hierarchical level are social needs, the wish for belonging, for association and acceptance by one's fellows, for giving and receiving friendship and love. Social link as a correlate of people's participation is anchored on this concept. People will participate because they need acceptance from those whom they are related with, otherwise, they will deny their participation.

Above the social needs are the ego needs, for the affirmation of the individual's identity and value. These are of two kinds; firstly, those that relate to self-esteem, self-confidence in mastery of the environment feeling of indifference and a sense of achievement and competence; and secondly, needs that relate to one's reputation in the eyes of others – the needs for status among peers, for recognition, appreciation and respect. Educational attainment as a variable is supported by this theory. While others may join because of what they could get, others join to maintain their status in the community. They are more concerned with the less concrete incentive. Thus, educated members find more satisfaction in personal benefits. Their educational qualification, expertise and skills provide them the recognition, appreciation and respect they crave for.

Finally, at the highest level are the needs for self-fulfillment, the drive towards realizing one's fullest potential, to continue one's self-development, to become creative. It is therefore conceived that an individual will continue to seek growth which is achieved in this study through attending seminars and trainings. Such an attendance relate with their participation in self-help projects.

Maslow suggests that human beings are largely self-motivated; it is difficult to motivate them except insofar as one can attempt to get them to achieve their own goals by directing efforts to the group goals. Most adults involved in community life are motivated by a mixture of self-interest and interest involved in the group cause.[1]

1 Abraham Maslow, Motivation and Personality, cited by Catherine Briscoe and David M. Thomas, Community Work: Learning and Supervision, (National Institute, Social Services Library, London, George Allen and Unwin Ltd., 1977), p. 84.

Resembling Maslow's but more on the point of personality development, Chris Argyris suggests that in one culture, typically, personality develops from an immature to mature state through changes in these aspects of the self:

1. from passivity to activity (doing for oneself rather than having others do for one)
2. from dependence to independence (from seeking direction to liking autonomy)
3. from inflexible to flexible behavior (ability to change and adopt)
4. from shallow interest to deep interest (finding satisfaction and rewards in doing something for its own sake)
5. from short perspective to long-term perspective (pursuing a long-term goal by a series of steps to the goal)
6. from accepting subordination to desiring equality or superiority to peers (seeking at least an equal voice in determining one's activity)
7. from lack of control to self-control (ability to direct one self without external control)[2]

This theory supports the contention of the researcher that age is a determinant of an individual's participation in self-help projects. As she/he develops and matures, she/he gains independence and control over his/her own self, thus, the more likely that she/he gains a better grasp of the community where she/he lives in and participates more in developmental activities.

The advocates of the Human Resource Theory hold out the promise

2 Chris Argyris, "The Individual and Organization: Some Problems of Mutual Adjustment", cited by Curt Tausky, Work Organization, Major Theoretical Perspectives, 2nd ed. (Illinois: F.E. Peacock Publisher, Inc., 1978), pp. 56-57.

of organizational productivity and heightened member satisfaction if emphasis is placed on the daily task people perform[3]. Participants become more active if they have conducive atmosphere in their fields of occupation. And if workers are not drained of their energies and time, their participation in self-help projects will be more active.

The Inter-actor Theory describes the mechanisms or processes by which actors act in situations of actions in relation to other actors. "Situations" here refers to the specific set of conditions that can generate, define and determine the course of a process[4]. Thus, the crucial aspect of the Expectancy Theory is that the selection of a course of action reflects the anticipated consequences of the action.

Likewise, Galbraith points out how participants can be influenced to contribute to team goals. The degree to which participants are willing to commit themselves to group tasks depends on the degree to which the group's performance is instrumental in satisfying their needs. This depends on how important they perceive them to be whether they believe they have the needed skills and whether their performance in the group will be evaluated or taken into account at the performance review. From this concept, it could be inferred that while it is true that some joiners are after the benefits they could get, some are more concerned as to whether they could contribute their skills, ideas and expertise, for them to be recognized, thus, gaining prestige and personal satisfaction.

---

3 Ibid, p.53

4 Joseph Berger, et.al., Sociological Theories in Progress, New Formulation, (California: Sage Publication, 1989), p.4

APPENDIX F

SAMPLE CONCEPTUAL FRAMEWORK

(CUI: 1995)

Conceptual Framework

The researcher conceptualized that personal characteristics and situational factors are related to an individual's level of participation in self-help projects. The aforementioned theories of motivation, personality development, the Human Resource Theory, Law of Associationism, Law of Effect, Inducement/Contribution Theory, Human Relations Theory and the rest reached a common point in supporting the variables indicated.

As mentioned, people's participation in self-help projects is determined by their personal characteristics. Age which is affected by an individual's maturity, experiences, and sense of independence has something to do with their extent of participation. Educational attainment is another variable. Level of perception and understanding of group endeavors are affected by one's educational background thus, participation on self-help projects varies.

Occupation, another correlate is believed to have a bearing on participation. The type of job one does as well as the demand for his/her time and energy would cause a variation in the participation in self-help projects. Household size is another factor. The number of members in the household has an effect on their economic and social conditions, thus, it will make a difference in their participation.

Membership in organizations may do the same. Exposure to similar experiences, benefits, roles and satisfaction from joining associations and clubs have something to do with their participation. Similarly, attendance in participatory-related activities with variation in terms of frequencies and kind of training attended may pose a difference in their participation.

Situational factors are conceived to be related with people's participation in self-help projects. Social link or the relationship one has within the group could spell a great significance. The number and kind of relationship one has would determine his/her participation in self-help projects.

The type of projects, on the other hand, could be one factor too. If an individual perceives a project to be more favorable on his part, she/he is inclined to participate more. Economic, social, environmental and cultural type of projects have different areas of priority, thus, difference in the participation is possible.

Individuals work for an object. Whether it be material, social or personal incentives, an individual participates if there is some benefit derived from a particular project. Hence, it is a significant determinant of people's participation in self-help projects.

One's time is a very valuable commodity. The quantity of time left for an individual to involve himself in self-help projects will in a way determine his participation.

People's participation which could either be active or inactive could be traced from the indicators used in the study. The higher the scores, the more active the participation is. The lower the scores, the less active is the participation.

This conceptualization is best represented through the following schema (Figure 1).

ERRATA SHEET

PARADIGM OF THE STUDY

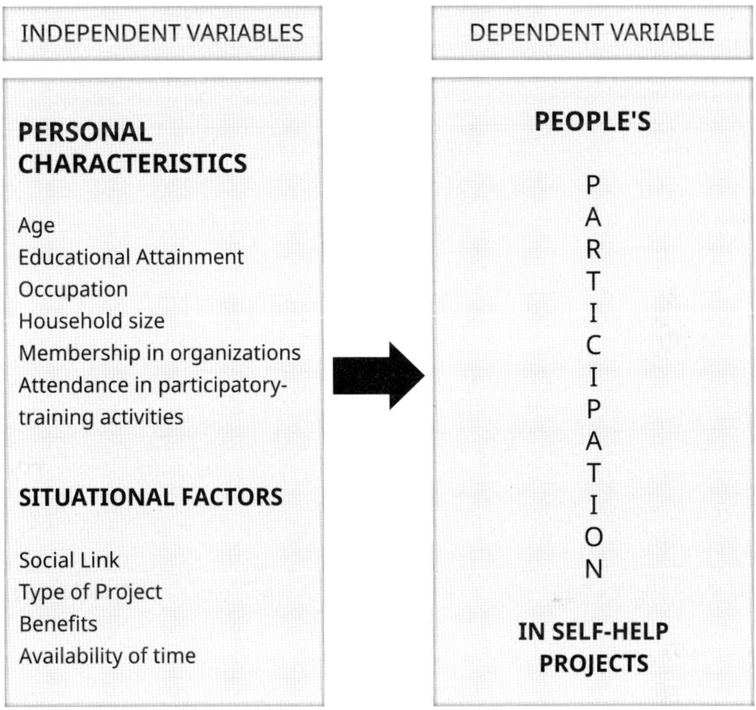

Appendix F's Figure 1. A schematic Diagram Showing the Relationship of the Independent and Dependent Variables

PARADIGM OF THE STUDY

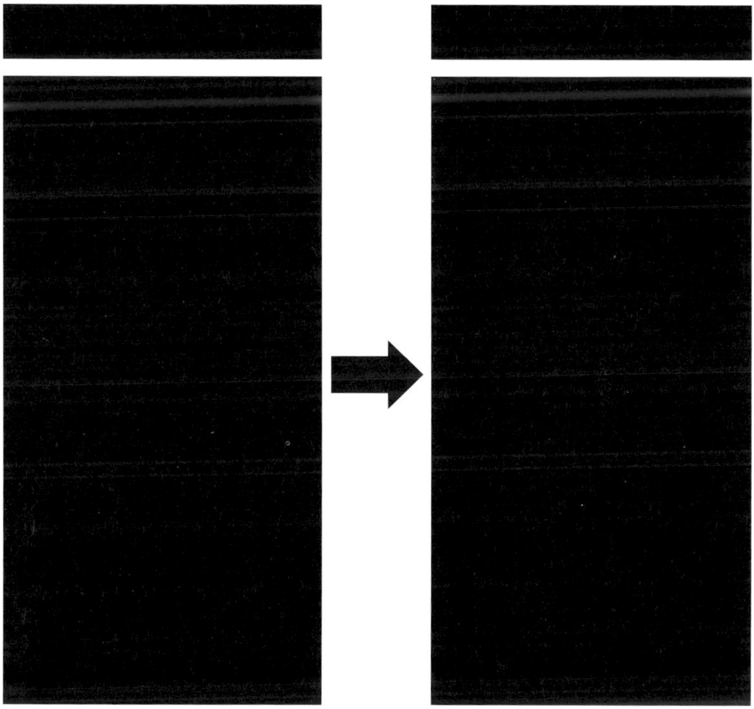

Appendix F's Figure 1. A schematic Diagram Showing the Relationship of the Independent and Dependent Variables

APPENDIX G

SAMPLE HYPOTHESES

"Before" and "After" Versions of Five Research Hypotheses (Salkind:1997)

BEFORE	AFTER
1. "Perceptions and attitudes positively relate to the manner in which the occupational activities are conducted."	1. "Fisherman who have a more positive attitude towards environmental preservation will also be less likely to use environmentally destructive fishing practices."
2. "The education of the person has some sort of relationship with mortality rate."	2. "The mortality rate found among highly educated persons will tend to be lower than that obtained for persons with a low level of educational attainment."
3. "Single persons have a lower death rate than those who are widowed."	3. "Controlling for age, single persons have a lower death rate than those who are widowed." Madrasah graduates will have a more favorable perception of job opportunities in the Middle East."
4. "There is significant correlation between the respondent's preference of Madrasah type of education and the...perception of job opportunities in the Middle-East."	4. "Farmer-recipients under the surplus land programme will have (a) higher incomes than the landless agricultural workers not covered by the programme but (b) lower incomes than farmer-owners who already have their own land (and who are therefore not covered by the program)."
5. "Farmer-recipients under the surplus land programme will have higher income than those farmers who do not come under the programme."	5. "Farmer-recipients under the surplus land programme will have (a) higher incomes than the landless agricultural workers not covered by the programme but (b) lower incomes than farmer-owners who already have their own land (and who are therefore not covered by the program)."

APPENDIX H

SAMPLE DEFINITION OF TERMS

(CUI: 1995)

Definition of Terms

For clarity, the following terms used in the study are conceptually and operationally defined:

Age is the number of years from birth of the respondents to their last birthday at the time of the interview. It was dichotomized as young or old. Respondents whose ages were below the mean were considered young while those whose ages were within or above the mean were considered old.

Attendance in Participatory-Training Activities refers the number of seminars or participatory-related activities such as pre-membership seminar, officership trainings, and others which a respondent attended. Respondents who attended four or more trainings were classified as with adequate attendance while those who attended three or less trainings were classified as with inadequate attendance.

Availability of Time refers to the respondent's extra time for participating in self-help projects. It was categorized as with sufficient or insufficient time. Those who have three or more hours/month were considered with sufficient time while those who have two hours or less/month were classified as with insufficient time.

Benefits are the incentives derived from participating in self-help projects. It was classified as material, social or personal[5]. In this study, benefits refer to increased income, better crop production, savings,

5 World Development Journal, "Participation's Place in Rural Development, " Vol.8, (Oxford, New York, 1980), pp. 219-221.

land/implements, loan opportunities, household commodities, farming tools/equipment. Social benefits refer to better health services, improved housing condition, better roads, safe water system, health centers and minimal illegal fishing. Personal benefits are better human relationship, additional knowledge, prestige and sense of power.

APPENDIX I

SAMPLE BIBLIOGRAPHY

(Tejero: 1995)

A. Books

Alfiler, Ma. Concepcion P. "Factors that Promote or Deter Popular Participation in Development: The Philippine Experience". **Introduction to Public Administration in the Philippines**. Edited by Victoria A. Bautista, Ma. Concepcion P. Alfiler, Danilo R. Reyes, Proserfina D. Tapales, Diliman, Quezon City, UP College of Public Administration. 1993.

Coleman, James S. "Half of the Sky in China". **Asian Woman**. Lucklow, India: Lucklow Publishing House. 1997.

Constantino, Letecia R. **Issues Without Tears: A Layman's Manual of Current Issues,** Vol. III (Quezon City: Karrel. Inc., 1989).

Guilford, J.P. and Benjamin Fruchter. **Fundamental Statistics in Psychology and Education.** London: McGraw-Hill, Ltd., 1973.

Heilbroner, Robert. **The Designs of Rural Development: Lessons from Africa.** Baltimore and London: The John Hopkins University Press. 1963.

Myrdal, Gunnar. **Asian Drama: An Inquiry into the Poverty of Nations.** New York: Pantheon House. 1968.

Palma, Cecilia-Munoz as cited by Ma. Teresa R. Robles. "Women in Constitution: A Better Deal". **Development Issues: Constitutional Response.** Florangel Rosario-Braid (Ed) Manila: National Book Store. 1986.

Panopio, Isabel S., Felicidad V. Cordero, Adelisa A. Raymundo. **General Sociology Focus in the Philippines**. Quezon City: KEN Incorporated. 1984.

Punzalan, Twila G. and Gabriel G. Uriarte. **Statistics: A Simplified Approach.** Manila: Rex Book Store. 1982.

Robles, Ma. Teresa R. "Women in Constitution: A Better Deal". **Development Issues: Constitutional Response**. Florangel Rosario-Braid. (Ed.) Manila; National Book Store. 1986.

Rola, Dionisia A. (Ed.). **Integrating Rural Development: Problems and Issues.** Quezon City: University of the Philippines Management Education Council. 1979.

Tirona, Gertie Ampil. **Empowering Woman: The Helena Z. Benitez Herstory.** Rapid Lithographic Inc. and the Helena Z. Benitez Heritage Foundation. 1995

Todaro, Michael P. **Economic Development in the Third World.** London: Longman. 1989.

"Introducion". **Development Issues: Constitutional Response.** Florangel Rosario-Braid (Ed.) Manila: National Book Store. 1986

The Reader's Digest Great Encyclopedic Dictionary. Vol. Three. London: The Reader's Digest Association. 1978.

Webster's II New Riverside University Dictionary. Boston: Houghton Mifflin Company, 1984.

B. Periodicals

Castillo, Gelia T. "The Changing Role for Women in Rural Societies: A Summary of Trends and Issues". A Summary Report of the Seminar Sessions Organized by the Fourth Congress for Rural Sociology, Torim, Poland. 1976.

Degler, C.N. "American Women in Social and Political Affairs: Change and Challenge". The Education of Women for Social and Political Leadership. A Symposium at Southern Methodist University. SMU Press. 1967.

Godt, Sue, et. al. Women in Development, **CUSO Forum**. March 1984.

Scott, Gloria. WID Briefing Note. (Draft) World Bank. October 6, 1983.

Seers, Dudley. "The Meaning of Development" A Paper Read at the 11th World Conference of the Society for International Development, New Delhi, India. November 14-17, 1969.

Tanada, Karen. "Realities of Filipino Women in Society". Samahan ng mga Manggagawang Kababaihan ng Luzon, Visayas at Mindanao **(SAMAKA-LUZVIMINDA).** December 1985.

Til, Jon Von and Sally Bould Til. "Citizen Participation in Social Policy: The End of the Cycle?" **Social Problems.** Winter 70. Vol. 17. No. 3.

Assessing the Realities of Filipino Women Workers in Trade Union Movement" **SAMAKA-LUZVIMINDA**, December 1985.

Overview of the Role of Women in Development. 1989 World Survey on the Role of Women in Development. United Nations Office at Vienna.

World Bank. Rural Development Sector Policy Paper. February 1975.

"North-South: A Programme for Survival". **Report of the Independent Commission on International Development Issues.** London: Pan Books. 1980.

Agriculture Canada: "Fact Sheet: **Women in Food Production**". World Food Day Secretariat. October 1984.

"The Teenage Mothers". Women in Development. **Development Forum**. UNA, New York. 1985.

Elements of Women's Economic Integration. **Project Indicators for the World Bank**. May 1982.

AID. A Seven-Country Suvey on the Role of Women in Rural Development. Prepared for the Agency for International Development under Contract No. AID/Ta C-73-41.

World Bank Annual Report. 1984.

Regional Development Council. **Medium Term Regional Development Plan,** 1990-1992. (Updated). Region VIII. Volume I. August 1990.

C. Unpublished Materials

Aguilar, Zosima B. "The Women Civic Organizations in Baguio City: Their Involvement in Community Development". Abstract. Baguio Central University. 1984.

Bascug, Marilyn Natividad M. "Decision Making and Leadership Patterns of Rural Women in Two Leyte Villages of the Philippines. Abstract. University of the Philippines at Los Banos, Laguna. November 1981.

Benitez, Agapita. "The Women's Organizations in Mountain Province: Their Involvement in Rural Development". Unpublished Master's Thesis. Baguio Central University, 1983.

Cruzado, V.T. "Leadership in Decision Making of the Barangay Council Members in Bukidnon". Unpublished Doctoral Dissertation. UPLB, Laguna . January 1977.

Evidente, Sister Ma. Asuncion G. O.C. "Development Orientation of Secondary School Administrators in Bicol". Unpublished Doctoral Dissertation. U.P. College of Educaton, Diliman, Quezon City. May 1974.

Gochingco, L. "Factors Influencing the Participation of Home

Economics Teachers in the Philippines". Unpublished Master's Thesis. Cornell University. 1961.

Lachica, Virginia Cortcz . "Professional Women and Their Contribution to Rural Development". Unpublished Master's Thesis. Don Mariano Marcos Memorial State University. November 1981.

Rabanal, Ernesto. "Guidance Activities Undertaken by Classroom Teachers in the Primary Grades of Cayupo, Nueva Ecija. "Unpublished Master's Thesis. Lyceum Northwestern College. Laoag City. 1972.

D. Other Sources

Minifacts on Filipino Women, National Commission on the Role of Filipino Women. 1992.

Socio-Economic Profile, Eastern Visayas (Region VIII). 1990.

1990 Census of Population, Socio-Economic and Demographic Characteristics, National Statistics Office, Manila.

"A Better World for All of Us". Development Education for the

Classroom, 1991, as cited by Dr. Gloria Salandaan, "Teacher Education for Tomorrow's Schools" (Mimeographed Copies

APPENDIX J

SAMPLE RESEARCH INSTRUMENTS

A. Questionnaire On Level Of Empowerment

(Tejero: 1995)

Directions: This is a self-assessment of how self-reliant and how empowered you are. Please select from the choices by underlining your answer. Please answer the questions truthfully. There are no right or wrong answers.

1. Can you define your own problems?	Always	Often	Sometimes	Never
2. Can you define the problems of your family?	Always	Often	Sometimes	Never
3. Are you able to give appropriate solutions to them?	Always	Often	Sometimes	Never
4. Do you see to the ultimate solution of your problems?	Always	Often	Sometimes	Never
5. Are you able to prioritize your needs and problems?	Always	Often	Sometimes	Never
6. Do you need help of others in solving your problems?	Always	Often	Sometimes	Never
7. Do you need help of others in doing your work?	Always	Often	Sometimes	Never
8. Do you always know what to do in case you are confronted with difficult situations in life?	Always	Often	Sometimes	Never
9. Do you need to be persuaded to join worthwhile activities?	Always	Often	Sometimes	Never

10. Do you exercise your own initiative in doing things for the common good?	Always	Often	Sometimes	Never
11. Are you wary of knowledge about?	Always	Often	Sometimes	Never
12. Are you able to make wise and timely decisions?	Always	Often	Sometimes	Never
13. Do you rely much on your own abilities than on others?	Always	Often	Sometimes	Never
14. Can you approach people with whom you need help?	Always	Often	Sometimes	Never
15. Do you always know what to do and where to go when confronted?	Always	Often	Sometimes	Never
16. With critical and crucial situations which need immediate decision?	Always	Often	Sometimes	Never

QUESTIONNAIRE ON ATTITUDERS

1. Are you able to articulate your thoughts?

0 1 2 3 4 5 6 7 8 9 10

I am not able to articulate my thoughts very well	I am well able to articulate my thoughts but	I am very much articulate with my thoughts

2. Can you act on your own?

0 1 2 3 4 5 6 7 8 9 10

I can't do anything on my own	I feel I can do things on my own but.....	I am confident to do things on my own.

3. Do you feel that you can help transform your environment into a pleasant place to live in?

0	1	2	3	4	5	6	7	8	9	10

I am totally helpless to do it	With the help of others I feel I can do it but	Through my own efforts and with the help of others I am confident we can do it

---

4. Do you consider yourself as somebody who is knowledgeable about things?

0	1	2	3	4	5	6	7	8	9	10

I am just an ignorant person	My knowledge is just enough for my own purposes.	I use my knowledge to help me and others live peacefully and progressively in society

---

5. Do you feel that you are doing something for the good of your community?

0	1	2	3	4	5	6	7	8	9	10

I am unable to do it because I am busy	I am unable to do it because I am busy	I devote most of my time doing things to help others in the community

---

6. Are the members in your community doing what they can to promote development in your area?

0	1	2	3	4	5	6	7	8	9	10

People are self - oriented	People do very little for the common good	People are doing their utmost to promote the general welfare.

7. What is your attitude towards your present condition in life?

0 1 2 3 4 5 6 7 8 9 10

I am the most unfortunate person on earth	I feel I am able to do things I want to do even if......	I am happy as I am

8. Do you have the notion that other people may need you to help in community activities?

0 1 2 3 4 5 6 7 8 9 10

I feel I am unimportant to them to bother about me.	I know people like me to join in community activities.	I have the feeling that people want me to join them and I'll just be glad to pitch in

9. How do you feel about changes taking place in your community

0 1 2 3 4 5 6 7 8 9 10

I want things as they are.	I want to see changes for the improvement of my community	Changes are steps towards progress and development and if ever my help will be needed I will be willing to oblige.

10. Do you have adequate experience in community building?

0 1 2 3 4 5 6 7 8 9 10

I am very inexperienced.	I have the experience but don't have the time	My experience is rich and I'm willing to my expertise.

11. Do you believe that being a woman has many disadvantages?

0 1 2 3 4 5 6 7 8 9 10

I feel very much inferior to men	inferior to men things equally good as men do.	Being a woman is a blessing. I love being one

12. How do men regard women in your locality?

0 1 2 3 4 5 6 7 8 9 10

Women are the to inferior sex and only useful when ey satisfy their needs and wants	Women's place is in the home taking care of their children and their men. Men love going me to a woman	Women are as capable and responsible as men They need to be loved and respected.

13. Do you feel discriminated against men whether in work or in society?

0 1 2 3 4 5 6 7 8 9 10

Employers choose men first than women. Women are only selected when there are no men available for the job.	Employers/People consider women on equal status with men but women sometimes have impediments like having baby.	There is no discrimination between men and women. Whoever is qualified is taken regardless of sex.

14. Would you rather be a man than a woman because of the injustices and unfairness to them?

0 1 2 3 4 5 6 7 8 9 10

Being a woman is being inferior	I like to be as I am although at times.....	Despite all odds, I still want to be what I am now, a woman.

APPENDIX K

SAMPLE INTERVIEW SCHEDULE

Interviewee's name______________ Interviewer______________

Home address__________________ Timestarter ______________

Date of Interview ______________ Time finished ____________

1. What is the meaning of environment? What composes it? (What does it include? How far does it extend?
2. What would you wish for, most of all, to improve your own life? Describe the kind of life that you consider ideal or best for you. What do you wish for your family?
3. What is most undesirable in your immediate environment? What will you do to improve this condition?
4. What conditions in the country should be improved? In your opinion, who is in the best position to take action toward improving these conditions in the country? What has this person/ group done to improve these conditions?
5. Farming and Livestock. Are our food resources producing enough to feed the people? What is being done to improve food production? What do you know about pesticides? How does it help in improving farming or agricultural production? Do you know of any harmful effects of pesticides? What are they? What projects has the government launched to improve the lot of farmers?...to improve farming ....to improve livestock raising? Are you involved in any of these?

6. Forestry. What are the country's problems about forestry? What projects have been initiated by the government and the private sector to solve these problems? In what ways can the loss of forests affect our lives adversely? What can you do to help solve these problems?
7. Mining. Does our country have enough mineral resources?

APPENDIX L

SAMPLE OBSERVATION SHEET

OBSERVATION SHEET for AFFECTIVE BEHAVIOR

(Fonollera:1997)

DIRECTIONS: Your role is to watch and listen for signs of the behavior described. Record Observations.

There are five (5) separate 10-minute observation and marking periods in each 90-minute visit to the room. Those are indicated by the headings I, II, III, IV, and V. During period I, spend the first 5 minutes observing the behavior of the students. In the next 5 minutes go down the list of items and place a plus (+) in the column beside all the items you saw occur. Place a minus (-) in the column for all items that did not occur. Place a zero (0) for all items which cannot make a discrimination. Each item should be considered and marked either with a +, -, or 0. A particular item is marked as many times as it occurs in a given column within the 10-minute observation period but only once for each student being observed.

Repeat this process for the second 10-minute period, marking in column II. Repeat for the third, fourth and fifths 10-minute periods, marking in columns III, IV and V, respectively. Please add the total number of +'s recorded in columns I through V for each student behavior and record in the column labeled TOT. There may be from 0 to 5 +'s times the number of students you are assigned to observe for each item.

APPENDIX M

SAMPLE BUSINESS RESEARCH ABSTRACT

Gerard George and Adam Jay Bock. 2009. **The Business Model in Practice and its Implications for Entrepreneurship Research**. University of Edinburgh Business School.

Abstract

While the term "business model" has gained widespread use in the practice community, the academic literature on this topic is fragmented and confounded by inconsistent definitions and construct boundaries. In this study, we review prior research and reframe the business model with an entrepreneurial lens. We report on a discourse analysis of 151 surveys of practicing managers to better understand their conceptualization of a business model. We find that the underlying dimensions of the business model are resource structure, transactive structure, and value structure, and discuss the nature and implications of dimensional dominance for firm characteristics and behavior. These findings provide new directions for theory development and empirical studies in entrepreneurship by linking the business model to entrepreneurial cognition, opportunity co-creation and organizational outcomes.

APPENDIX N

TIPS FOR PRE-ORAL AND FINAL DEFENSES

1. Write a prayer that will best suit your intentions and purposes.
2. Make sure your research paper is well edited and printed.
3. Be ready to explain everything that appears in your research paper.
4. Get the meaning of unfamiliar and difficult words in your paper. Be sure you understand everything that you have included . Chances are, you will be made to explain important citations in your text.
5. Although you are not expected to memorize your book from cover-to-cover, you are expected to know the many significant details about your study. Answers to specific details such as your problem at hand, your research design, research methodology, respondents, research instruments, sampling procedure, scoring of data, etc. should be within your fingertips.
6. Know your statistical computations and how they are interpreted. Your statistician will be able to assist you in this aspect.
7. Be cordial and respectful in answering the questions. Courteous language has always a place in intellectual exchanges.
8. The secretary records the suggestions made by the panelists. A copy is given to you after your defense. Read the suggestions before you leave. Clarify suggestions which are somewhat ambiguous to you while the panelists are still in tact. When they disperse you will have a hard time seeing them individually.

9. The time allowed for the revision of your manuscript based on the suggestions is usually two weeks. Set your target date for the revisions and do it in record time. Leaving your work to some other time is procrastination. When this sets in, you will not be able to finish your work as scheduled. Time is an important commodity which you should not waste.

10. You are advised to submit your revised and approved research proposal before undertaking data gathering.

11. Timeliness and freshness of your data and findings are crucial factors. If you do not act on time, your research will be overtaken by events and everything will become obsolete without you even knowing it.

BIBLIOGRAPHY

A. BOOKS

Argyris, Chris. 1978. "The Individual and Organization: Some Problems of Mutual Adjustment" In Curt Tausky. Work Organization, Major Theoretical Perspectives. 2nd ed. Illinois: F.E Peacock Publisher, Inc.

Ary, Donald, et al. 1979. Introduction to Research in Education.2nd ed. New York: Holt, Rinehart and Winston, Inc.

Bondoc, Victoriana P., Rochella C. David, Alma B. Gueco,, Lyn V. Lansangan, Edgar L. Manabat, Ma. Irelyn P. Tamayo, Imelda P. Macaspac. 2014. Action Research Made Easy (A Practical Guide to the Preparation of Action Research in Education) Manila: Lorimar Publishing, Inc.

Broto, Antonio S. 2003. Statistics Made Simple. Manila. MELBROS, Inc.

Campbell, Williams G. S.V Bablou and C. Slade. 1982. Form and Style: Thesis, Reports, Term Papers (8th ed. Boston: Houghton Mifflin.

Creswell, J. W. 2008. Educational Research: Planning, Conducting and Evaluating Quantitative and Qualitative Research. 3rd Ed. New Jersey: Pearson.

Douglas A. Lind. William G. Marchal. Samuel A. Wathen. 2010. Basic Statistics for Business & Economics. Seventh Edition. Philippines: McGraw-Hill International Edition.

Egipto, Joel Joseph. 2011. Writing Business Letters. Manila: REX Book Store, Inc.

Ferguson, George A. 1971. Statistical Analysis in Psychology and Education. 3rd ed. Tokyo: McGraw-Hill Kogakusha, Ltd.

Fonollera, Maura B. 1993. Developing Competencies in Research Writing. Pasig City: Filipinas International Technology Services, Inc.

Fox, David J. 1969. The Research Process in Education. New York: Holt, Rinehart and Winston, Inc.

Fraenkel, J. R. and N. E. Walters. 2008. How to Design and Evaluate Research in Education. 7th Ed. Boston: McGraw-Hill.

Kerlinger, Fred N. 1973. Foundations of Behavioral Research. 2nd ed. New York: Holt, Rinehart and Winston, Inc.

Kotler, P. (2003). Marketing Management (11th ed.). Upper Saddle River, NJ: Pearson Education, Inc., Prentice Hall.

Lehmann, D. R. Gupta, S., and Seckel, J. (1997). Market Research. Reading, MA: Addison-Wesley.

Neto, John Sydenstricker. Research Design and Mixed-Method Approach. A Hands-On Experience. http: trochin.human.cornell.edu/tutorial/sydenstricker/balsa.html.

MacMillan, J. H. (2008). Educational Research: Fundamentals for the Consumer. 5th Ed. Boston: Pearson.

Manuel, Bienvinido B. and Paz C. Medel. 1985. A Practical Guide to Methodology of Research and Thesis Writing.

McGuigan, F.J. 1978. Experimental Psychology. 3rd ed. Manila: National Book Store.

Mueller, Daniel J. 1996. Measuring Social Attitudes. New York and London: Teachers College Press, Columbia University.

Reitz, Joseph H. 1981. Human Behavior in Organizations. Manila: Golden Art Publishing Corporation.

Salkind, Neil J. Exploring Research. 1997. 3rd ed. New Jersey: Prentice-Hall.

Sampa, Elias M. 2012. Rudiments of Qualitative Designs and Analysis. Manila: REX Book Store, Inc.

Sarno, Emerlita G. Magsajo. 2010. Tips and Techniques in Writing Research. Manila: REX Book Store, Inc.

Sekaran Uma and Roger Bougie. 2013. " Research Methods for Business: A skill-Building Approach" Sixth Edition. United Kingdom: John Wiley and Sons Ltd.

Sprinthall, Richard C. 1994. Basic Statistical Analysis. Boston: Allyn and Bacon.

Thorndike, Edward Lee. 1985. "The Theories of Learning" In Gaudencio Aquino and Perpetua Razon. Advanced Psychology, A Contemporary Approach. Manila: Garcia Publishing House.

Travers, M.W Robert. 1978. An Introduction to Educational Research. 4th ed. New York: MacMillan Publishing Co. Inc.

Tuckman, Bruce W. 1988. Conducting Educational Research. Orlando, Florida: Harcourt Brace Jovanovich, Inc.

Turubian, Kate L. 1980. A Manual for Writers of Term Papers, Theses, and Dissertations. 4th ed. Chicago and London: The University Chicago Press.

Tungpalan, Ma. Teresea V. 1997. Handbook for Researchers. Diliman, Quezon City: Research and Extension Development Office, College of Social Work and Community Development, University of the Philippines.

Vockell, Edward L. 1983. Educational Research. New York: MacMillan Publishing Co. Inc.

Weirsman, William. 1975. Research Methods in Education. 2nd ed. Illinois: F.E Peacock Publishing Inc.

B. Periodicals

Costello, Michael A. 1997. "Look Before You Leap: Some Reflections on Hypotheses Formulation in the Social Sciences" in PSSC Social Science Information. Vol. 25, No. 2.

Gogolin, L. and P.S Swartz. 1992. "A Quantitative and Qualitative Inquiry into the Attitudes Toward Science of Nonscience College Students." Journal of Research in Science.

C. Other Sources

American Psychological Association. 1983. Publication Manual of the American Psychological Association. 3rd ed. Washington, D.C.

De Vault, Gigi. (2014). Market Research Data Analysis

National Higher Education Research Agenda (1998-2007). Commission on Higher Education. Pasig City.

Saavedra, Elisa A. 1997. "Research Proposal and Thesis Writing: A Suggested Guide" Seminar on Thesis and Dissertation Writing and Advising, San Carlos University, Cebu City.

Seminar Handouts: 1997. The Deductive Mode of Research in a Quantitative Study", "The Inductive Mode of Research in a Qualitative Study", A Checklist of Questions for Designing Survey Method", A Compendium of Data Collection Approaches in Qualitative Research. Thesis and Dissertation Writing and Advising, San Carlos University, Cebu City.

Tejero, Erlinda G. 1999. "Guidelines for Writing Thesis Proposals and Dissertation Protocols. Unpublished Material.

Writing a Thesis/Dissertation Proposal. 2000. Workshop Materials and Handouts. Philippine Social Science Council, Inc.

D. Online Sources

- Dontingney, Eric, Types of Business Research Method. Retrived at http://smallbusiness.chron.com/tupes-business-research-methods-57582.html

- Globio, Erwin M.(2014)."Summary, Conclusions, Recommendations," Thesis and Dissertation Writing Council. Available at: https://www.facebook.com/thesisconsultants

  Johnson, Doug. Plagiarism-Proofing Assignments.. Phi Delta Kappan, Vol. 85, No. 07 (March 2004).). Adapted from a chapter in the book Teaching Right from Wrong in the Digital Age (Linworth, 2003)

- Lee, Sherrie. 2013. "Researching Identities of English Learners". University of Waikato, New Zealand. Retrieved from http://www.linkedin.com/in/orangecanton

  Penn Libraries. ESE Senior Design Project.. Retrieved from http://gethelp.library.upenn.edu/guides/engineering/ee/plagiarize.html

  100 Research Paper Topics. 2014. Midway College, Midway, KY.

  http://www.midway.edu/library/topics

  Sreejesh, S., Mohapatra, S., Anusree, M. R. (2014). Business Research Process: An Orientation. Available at: http://www.springer.com/978-319-005386

- "Summary". Research on the Economic Impact of Cooperatives. Report Prepared by University of Wisconsin Center for Cooperatives. Available at: http://reic.uwcc.wisc.edu/ summary/

- Taylor, D 2008 "The Literature Review: A few Tips on conducting it. Health Sciences Writing Center", University of Toronto, available at The Literature Review: A Few Tips On Conducting It. Health Sciences Writing Center,University of Toronto available at http://www.writing.utoronto.ca/advice/specific-types-of-writing/lifeshare-review

- Cronholm, Stefan and Andress Hialmarsson, 2011 "Experiences from sequential use of Mixed Method" The Electronc Journal of Business Research Methods Vol. 9, Issue June 2 2011 pp 87.95 availed at www.ejbrm.com http://www.academia.edu/46723319/Review of Literature and studies-sampling

About the Authors

ASTERIO T. MIRANDA, JR. is an associate professor of the College of Business Administration of Keimyung University(KMU), South Korea. He holds a doctorate degree in Extension Education, with Agribusiness Management as cognate, from the University of the Philippines at Los Banos (UPLB), Laguna, Philippines. Before his stint in South Korea, he was also an associate professor and chair of the Department of Agribusiness and Agricultural Economics of the College of Agriculture, Fisheries and Natural Resources, University of Eastern Philippines (UEP), University Town, Northern Samar. He had published research papers and articles in local and international publications. Dr. Miranda was a scholar of the UEP Faculty Development Program for his master's degree in Business Administration and for his Doctorate degree, he was awarded full scholarship by the Department of Agriculture-Bureau of Agricultural Research (DA-BAR) under the NARDSAF. He was tapped by the World Council for Credit Union as Technical Advisor of a project in Southern Afghanistan which was tasked to organize and develop Islamic Investment and Finance Cooperatives, under the auspices of USAID.

JUNETH LOURDES FIEL-MIRANDA is an associate professor of accounting and other business related subjects at Keimyung Adams College (KAC) of the Keimyung University in South Korea. She has been an associate professor at the Catholic University of Daegu, South Korea, teaching accounting courses. She graduated with distinction from Western Leyte College for her undergraduate degree in Commerce, and received her Master in Business Administration (MBA) degree from the University of Eastern Philippines, and finished her Doctorate degree in Management major in Human Resources Management at the University of San Jose Recoletos, Cebu City, Philippines. She successfully hurdled the Professional Board Examination for Certified Public Accountants (CPA). For over two decades, she worked as Associate Professor of accounting and was involved in the development and implementation of the four-year degree program in cooperatives; conducted research and extension activities; and took an active role in the establishment of a collaborative linkage between the University of Eastern Philippines and the Grameen Foundation-Australia.

ERLINDA GALERO-TEJERO held the academic rank of Associate Professor 4 and was also designated as Technical Assistant to the Vice President for Administration (VPA) of the University of Eastern Philippines, University Town, and Northern Samar. She finished her BEED, MA, and Ph. D. degrees from the said university where she worked. She completed the Advanced Training Program in the Teaching of Reading from the University of the Philippines, Diliman, Quezon City as a scholarship grantee. She wrote and published professional articles in local, national, and international publications. A seasoned and experienced educator, she has to her credit 38 years of fruitful teaching experience in all levels of the educational hierarchy, from preschool to the Graduate School. In her retirement years, she travels a lot to see local scenes and sights. Her travel to Sydney Australia opened up a lot of experiences and opportunities for her.

RESEARCH PERSPECTIVES IN BUSINESS

발행일	2018년 12월 01일 초판 1쇄
지은이	ASTERIO T. MIRANDA, JR.,Ph.D. JUNETH LOURDES F. MIRANDA, CPA, D.M. ERLINDA G. TEJERO, Ph.D
발행인	송자영
발행처	초아출판사
주소	서울시 성북구 정릉로 36길 41
전화	070-8739-0036
팩스	0504-178-5627
E-mail	choapublish@hanmail.net
디자인	에이카드

ISBN 979-11-88425-06-8
정가 20,000원